DATE DUE

2

AUG 1 5 1980

WOMEN AND WRITING

BOOKS BY VIRGINIA WOOLF

The Voyage Out, 1915
Night and Day, 1919
Kew Gardens, 1919
Monday or Tuesday, 1921
Jacob's Room, 1922
The Common Reader: First Series, 1925
Mrs. Dalloway, 1925
To the Lighthouse, 1927
Orlando, 1928
A Room of One's Own, 1929
The Waves, 1931
Letter to a Young Poet, 1932
The Second Common Reader, 1932
Flush, 1933
The Years, 1937
Three Guineas, 1938
Roger Fry: A Biography, 1940
Between the Acts, 1941
The Death of the Moth and Other Essays, 1942
A Haunted House and Other Short Stories, 1944
The Moment and Other Essays, 1947
The Captain's Death Bed and Other Essays, 1950
A Writer's Diary, 1954
Virginia Woolf and Lytton Strachey: Letters, 1956
Granite and Rainbow, 1958
Contemporary Writers, 1965
Collected Essays (4 vols.) 1967
Mrs. Dalloway's Party, 1973
The Letters of Virginia Woolf. Vol. I: 1888–1912, 1975
Freshwater, 1976
Moments of Being, 1976
The Letters of Virginia Woolf. Vol. II: 1912–1922, 1976
The Diary of Virginia Woolf. Vol. I: 1915–1919, 1977
Books and Portraits, 1977
The Pargiters: The Novel-Essay Portion of *The Years,* 1977
The Letters of Virginia Woolf. Vol. III: 1923–1928, 1977
The Letters of Virginia Woolf. Vol. IV: 1929–1931, 1978
The Diary of Virginia Woolf. Vol. II: 1920–1924, 1978
The Letters of Virginia Woolf. Vol. V: 1932–1935, 1979
Women and Writing, 1979
The Diary of Virginia Woolf. Vol. III: 1925–1930, 1980

Virginia Woolf

Women and Writing

EDITED AND WITH AN INTRODUCTION BY

Michèle Barrett

HARCOURT BRACE JOVANOVICH

NEW YORK AND LONDON

Printed in the United States of America

First published in England by The Women's Press Ltd

LIBRARY OF CONGRESS CATALOGING IN PUBLICATION DATA

Woolf, Virginia Stephen, 1882–1941.
Virginia Woolf, women and writing.
1. English literature—Women authors—History and
criticism—Addresses, essays, lectures.
2. Women— Addresses, essays, lectures.
3. Women authors—England—Addresses, essays, lectures.
I. Barrett, Michèle. II. Title.
III. Title: Women and writing.
PR6045.072A6   1980   820'.9'9287   79-3371
            ISBN 0-15-193775-3
                0-15-693658-5 pbk.

First American edition 1980
A B C D E F G H I J

Contents

WOMEN AND WRITING

Introduction

> To write, or read, or think, or to inquire,
> Would cloud our beauty, and exhaust our time,
> And interrupt the conquests of our prime,
> Whilst the dull manage of a servile house
> Is held by some our utmost art and use.
>
> Lady Winchilsea

This verse, written by a woman born in 1661, was quoted by Virginia Woolf in the book she published in 1929 on the subject of 'women and fiction'. Exactly fifty years after the publication of *A Room of One's Own* we find ourselves still debating the questions she raised there. What barriers, both inward and outward, do women face in attempting to produce literature? How do these barriers affect the character of the work they produce? What are the consequences, for the woman author, of historical changes in the position of women in society? In *A Room of One's Own* and in her critical essays Virginia Woolf developed a general theoretical account of women's literary work and attempted a detailed critical assessment of many individual authors. This subject was for her of life-long interest and it informs a major part of her critical work. Yet the arguments of *A Room of One's Own* and of *Three Guineas* (1938) have yet to be thoroughly debated and assessed. These two extended essays provide the background against which we should read the shorter works printed here.

Virginia Woolf's critical essays have been somewhat neglected since her death in 1941. In her lifetime she was regarded as one of the foremost critics of her day: she was a regular reviewer for *The Times Literary Supplement* and other journals, and T. S. Eliot claimed that she was 'the centre of the literary life of London'. This reputation has faded. Certainly Woolf is regarded as an important figure in the twentieth-century development of the novel, and her fiction has attracted an enormous critical literature. Her life, too, has generated great interest, both before and after the publication of Quentin Bell's influential biography in 1972. In some cases a somewhat sensational interest in her life, and in her role as *doyenne* of 'Bloomsbury', has replaced the serious attention her work might otherwise have received.

It is, perhaps, no coincidence that the development of this uneven reputation has been one in which her work as an essayist and critic has been neglected. To some extent literary criticism is imbued, more apparently than is a novel, with the attitudes of a particular time; it tends to fade with the death of the generation in which it was written. Yet in Virginia Woolf's case there may be another reason. Critics of her novels have consistently emphasized their supposedly 'feminine' and 'domestic' character, and indeed one critic makes for us the link between the novels and the essays. 'I doubt,' writes G. S. Fraser in his study of *The Modern Writer and His World* (Penguin, 1970), 'from her own writings, whether Mrs Woolf was any more capable of following an abstract philosophical argument than Clarissa Dalloway.' Such a remark is not so likely to be made of a male writer. Such judgements are perhaps more easily made of a woman who invades not only the arena of creativity (for which there are major precedents in the nineteenth-century novel), but also presumes to enter, as fewer women have done, the sphere of criticism, argument and theory. Virginia

Woolf was herself acutely aware of them. In 1932, when she was working on *Three Guineas* and putting together her second collection of essays, she wrote in her diary: 'I must go on with the *Common Reader* – for one thing, by way of proving my credentials.' The anticipation of adverse criticism must have led to a defensiveness on her part, and indeed it is worth quoting her uncannily accurate prediction of the fate of *A Room of One's Own*, from her 1929 diary:

> I will here sum up my impressions before publishing *A Room of One's Own*. It is a little ominous that Morgan [E. M. Forster] won't review it. It makes me suspect that there is a shrill feminine tone in it which my intimate friends will dislike. I forecast, then, that I shall get no criticism, except of the evasive jocular kind, from Lytton [Strachey], Roger [Fry] and Morgan; that the press will be kind and talk of its charm and sprightliness; also I shall be attacked for a feminist and hinted at for a Sapphist. . . . I am afraid it will not be taken seriously. Mrs Woolf is so accomplished a writer that all she says makes easy reading . . . this very feminine logic . . . a book to be put in the hands of girls. I doubt that I mind very much. . . . It is a trifle, I shall say; so it is; but I wrote it with ardour and conviction.

Virginia Woolf's desire to prove her intellectual credentials did not necessarily find support from those of her immediate circle who often praised her creative genius. The charge of shrillness which she feared in connection with *A Room of One's Own* has more frequently been levelled against *Three Guineas*. Although *The Times Literary Supplement* greeted this work with great praise, suggesting that 'This brilliant and searching pamphlet might mark an epoch in the world's history', the reviewer perciypiently foresaw that 'Many readers of this book will applaud, others grind their teeth'. In fact the grinders of teeth included many of those to whom

3

she looked for personal and literary reassurance: 'my own friends have sent me to Coventry over it', she noted. Her husband Leonard was 'less excited than I hoped' and her sister Vanessa 'highly ambiguous'. It might be argued that this lack of support was not solely related to the arguments, which are admittedly contentious, Virginia Woolf puts forward in *Three Guineas*. Indeed Q. D. Leavis pronounced in her review of it that there was no use, in the field of speculation about further female emancipation, for 'the non-specialist like Mrs Woolf' (*Scrutiny*, September 1938). It is perhaps small wonder that Virginia Woolf tried to make a virtue from the necessity of her isolation, as when she noted in her diary:

> I do my best work and feel most braced with my back to the wall. It's an odd feeling though, writing against the current: difficult entirely to disregard the current.

Virginia Woolf herself was aware of the connections between her fiction and non-fiction work, and indeed regarded *The Years* (1937) and *Three Guineas* as 'one book'. Critics have tended to separate them, emphasizing the technical and aesthetic characteristics of the novels and thereby losing much of their social and political significance. In publishing this selection of her critical work on women and writing we hope not only to provide a convenient volume but to clarify the relation between Woolf's critical work and her novels. The present selection covers general essays on women and writing and discussions of the work of individual women who form part of the female literary tradition. It is not a comprehensive collection of her work on this topic, but aims to give an indication of her general arguments and approach. Most of the essays here have been published, in Woolf's lifetime and posthumously, in the various Hogarth Press editions of her essays. Some, however, are more difficult to obtain at present, since they otherwise would exist only as reviews (often anonymous) or

4

articles in *The Times Literary Supplement* and other periodicals. A note of publication details is given at the beginning of each essay.

Virginia Woolf's analysis of literature
Virginia Woolf's approach to the question of women and fiction, about which she wrote extensively, polemically, and in a profoundly feminist way, was grounded in a general theory of literature. She argued that the writer was the product of her or his historical circumstances, and that material conditions were of crucial importance. Secondly, she claimed that these material circumstances had a profound effect on the psychological aspects of writing, and that they could be seen to influence the nature of the creative work itself.

Writing, Virginia Woolf asserts prosaically in *A Room of One's Own,* is based upon material conditions:

. . . these webs are not spun in mid-air by incorporeal creatures, but are the work of suffering human beings, and are attached to grossly material things, like health and money and the houses we live in.

These material things are ironically explored in her own case, in the essay 'Professions for Women':

. . . when I came to write, there were very few material obstacles in my way. Writing was a reputable and harmless occupation. The family peace was not broken by the scratching of a pen. No demand was made upon the family purse. For ten and sixpence one can buy paper enough to write all the plays of Shakespeare – if one has a mind that way. Pianos and models, Paris, Vienna and Berlin, masters and mistresses, are not needed by a writer. The cheapness of writing paper is, of course, the reason why women have succeeded as writers before they have succeeded in the other professions.

The more general argument she puts forward is that women have been constrained, and prevented from writing, by circumstances in which they were deprived of education and denied access to publishing. Most importantly perhaps, they were deprived of the right to make a living by their writing. In *A Room of One's Own* she describes with irritation how she was forbidden entry to an 'Oxbridge' library because she was a woman, and she stresses women's discouraging situation (prior to the Married Women's Property Acts):

> . . . in the first place to earn money was impossible for them, and in the second, had it been possible, the law denied them the right to possess what money they earned.

All these factors, she claims, created a situation in which women were virtually prevented from producing literature. In her correspondence about 'The Intellectual Status of Women' with Desmond MacCarthy (alias 'Affable Hawk') in the *New Statesman* (1920) she writes:

> To account for the complete lack not only of good women writers but also of bad women writers I can conceive no reason unless it be that there was some external restraint upon their powers.

and she goes on to quote J. A. Symonds on the case of Sappho:

> Several circumstances contributed to aid the development of lyric poetry in Lesbos. The customs of the Aeolians permitted more social and domestic freedom than was common in Greece. Aeolian women were not confined to the harem like Ionians, or subjected to the rigorous discipline of the Spartans. While mixing freely with male society, they were highly educated and accustomed to express their sentiments to an extent unknown elsewhere in history – until, indeed, to the present time.

In considering the effect of women's social situation on their writing Virginia Woolf stresses the important differences in the opportunities open for women of different social classes and at different periods of history. Up until the end of the seventeenth century it was only eccentric women from the aristocracy, like the Duchess of Newcastle and Lady Winchilsea, who were able, surreptitiously, to 'dabble' in writing. With Aphra Behn, the first woman (albeit not a very respectable one, she notes) to earn a living by writing, the field opened for the middle-class woman who could succeed in gaining some kind of access to an education and the world of literature. Even this hard-won education, Virginia Woolf stresses, was available only to 'the daughters of educated men', and was not open to women (or men) of the working class.

Virginia Woolf was herself extremely conscious of the disadvantage she suffered in not being formally educated, as her brothers had been as a matter of course. She wrote an essay entitled 'On Not Knowing Greek' and we find throughout her work an awareness of the expense that was lavished on the education of boys while their sisters languished under unsatisfactory private tuition and self-taught programmes of reading. At times this issue is dealt with lightly, as in the *New Statesman* correspondence where she challenges Arnold Bennett to produce fifty male poets who are superior to Sappho. 'If he will publish their names,' she continues.

> I will promise, as an act of that submission which is so dear to my sex, not only to buy their works but, so far as my faculties allow, to learn them by heart.

Yet it is clear from *Three Guineas* that she took this issue very seriously indeed. She argues in support of women's colleges, despite her hostility to academic hierarchies, since she saw them as the only chance for women to acquire independence and the right to earn their own living. They offered the possibility of a new kind of education, one that was not concerned to teach

> the arts of dominating other people . . . the arts of ruling, of killing, of acquiring land and capital.

Later on in *Three Guineas* Virginia Woolf stresses the need to challenge not only the exclusion of women from formal education, but the arguments and 'knowledge' used to legitimate this exclusion. She quotes Bertrand Russell's remark that

> Anyone who desires amusement may be advised to look up the tergiversations of eminent craniologists in their attempts to prove from brain measurements that women are stupider than men.

Virginia Woolf's explanation of this lies in the extent to which science was manipulated in the interests of fathers who wished to stave off the independence of their daughters that would result if they were allowed to be educated and earn their own living. 'Science', Woolf concludes, 'is not sexless; she is a man, a father, and infected too.'

Virginia Woolf's arguments about education do not directly reduce the writer to a mere product of prevailing social forces. 'The politician', she notes with disagreement, 'says that a writer is the product of the society in which he lives, as a screw is the product of a screw machine.' What she is arguing is a rather more complex and subtle point, but can be summarized in the idea that 'intellectual freedom depends upon material things'. The importance of these material things, as far as literature is concerned, is principally that they determine the writer's angle of vision. This point is made clearly in 'The Leaning Tower', a paper read to the Brighton Worker's Educational Association in 1940, and reprinted in *The Moment*. The perspective of the writer is linked to education, and beyond that to social class:

. . . if you look closely you will see that almost every writer who has practised his art successfully had been taught it. He has been taught it by about eleven years of education – at private schools, public schools, and universities. He sits upon a tower raised above the rest of us; a tower built first on his parents' station, then on his parents' gold. It is a tower of the utmost importance; it decides his angle of vision; it affects his power of communication.

This line of thinking, when Virginia Woolf is considering the specific situation of women writers, leads her to stress their relegation to a private world of home and family. We find a stress on the domestic isolation, the narrow social experience, of women writers, recurring many times in the essays printed here. Virginia Woolf speculates on the effect Jane Austen's fame might have had on her writing, had she lived long enough to benefit from it:

Had she lived a few more years only . . . She would have stayed in London, dined out, lunched out, met famous people, made new friends, read, travelled, and carried back to the quiet country cottage a hoard of observations to feast upon at leisure . . .

All this would not merely have added to her life, it would necessarily have enriched the scope of her novels, and Woolf argues that

She would have devised a method, clear and composed as ever, but deeper and more suggestive, for conveying not only what people say, but what they leave unsaid . . .

Virginia Woolf makes a comparable argument in the case of George Eliot who, she argues, escaped from Victorian morality (by living with the married George Lewes) only at the expense of an equally restrictive social censure and ostracism. Several times she quotes Eliot's painful awareness of her unacceptable social status:

> I wish it to be understood, that I should never invite anyone to come and see me who did not ask for the invitation

and comments that George Eliot thereby '. . . lost the power to move on equal terms unnoted among her kind; and the loss for a novelist was serious.'

Such strictures on conventionally immoral behaviour were, of course, applied in all their severity only to women and Virginia Woolf drily draws our attention to the life of Tolstoy at this period – philandering around Europe collecting the uncensored experience of life which was later to be the material on which *War and Peace* was based.

Some of the same observations apply to Virginia Woolf's consideration of Elizabeth Barrett Browning, and the effect of her peculiarly female invalidish isolation:

> It cannot be doubted that the long years of seclusion had done her irreparable damage as an artist. She had lived shut off, guessing at what was outside, and inevitably magnifying what was within.

In all these cases it is plain that to Virginia Woolf it is the *social* situation of the female writer that, to some extent at least, determines the nature of the work produced, and here lies the crux of her argument. It is an argument which is built up through detailed comment and observation, and even in *A Room of One's Own*, where it is most explicitly and thoroughly argued, it takes the form of an allusive, semi-fictional form of writing. This should not lead us into denying its logic or coherence; in her work as a whole we find many of the major elements of a highly developed feminist critical theory. For not only does she consider the nature of women's own literary production, she also covers the complex questions of the critical reception of texts by women authors, when criticism was in the hands of men, and the image of women presented in the predominantly male literary tradition.

Virginia Woolf draws attention to the condescending attitude of male critics towards women writers, and the inevitable effect this had on their work. Of course many writers tried to escape this prejudice by using male pseudonyms, but nonetheless it could not be evaded. Its influence is discernible in the very texture of the writing, as she notes in *A Room of One's Own*:

> One has only to skim those old forgotten novels and listen to the tone in which they were written to divine that the writer was meeting criticism; she was saying this by way of aggression, or that by way of conciliation.

Such bias, to Virginia Woolf an aesthetically undesirable element in a work of literature, was the inevitable consequence of the general climate of opinion with regard to women who challenged the narrow domestic lives prescribed for them. Another way in which this image of women was perpetuated, she argued, was in the representation of women in works by male writers. She makes the point that this representation traditionally took the form of a mirror-image of the position of women in real life. In discussing the conventional representation of women in literature, she comments

> Some of the most inspired words, some of the most profound thoughts fall from her lips; in real life she could hardly read, could scarcely spell, and was the property of her husband.

'Almost without exception,' she notes, women are 'shown in their relation to men.'

The force of Woolf's arguments is perhaps strongest when she considers the obstacles faced by women writers. These obstacles, she argues, are 'immensely powerful', yet 'difficult to define', and yet she precisely does try to define them in relation to her own writing in the essay 'Professions for Women'. Those same attitudes under which the great Victorian women novelists laboured have not evaporated, simply through formal changes in the possibilities open to women. In the present day, she asks rhetorically:

> Outwardly, what is simpler than to write books? Outwardly, what obstacles are there for a woman rather than for a man? Inwardly, I think, the case is very different; she still has many ghosts to fight, many prejudices to overcome.

In this essay Virginia Woolf suggests that the two main obstacles are the 'Angel in the House' and the difficulty of 'telling the truth about my own experiences as a body'; effectively this means rejecting the ideal, pure image of woman, and frankly exploring sexuality and the unconscious. Under the image of the 'Angel in the House' she summons up the ideal, self-sacrificing woman who

> was so constituted that she never had a mind or a wish of her own, but preferred to sympathize always with the minds and wishes of others.

In the earlier version of this essay (a draft of a speech given to a women's organization in 1931, and reprinted in *The Pargiters*, 1978) Virginia Woolf adds that this ideal of womanhood was accepted by both men and women

> for reasons I cannot now go into – they have to do with the British Empire, our colonies, Queen Victoria, Lord Tennyson, the growth of the middle class and so on

and she adds that it was addressed in literature 'in a style which to me is really disgusting'.

In the essay Virginia Woolf finally slays the Angel by throwing her inkpot at her, only to encounter the second problem, that of sexuality. Again this is presented allusively, in the image of the writer in a state of trance:

> She was letting her imagination sweep unchecked round every rock and cranny of the world that lies submerged in the depths of our unconscious being. . . . And then there was a smash. There was an explosion. There was foam and confusion . . . she had thought of something, something about the body, about the passions which it was unfitting for her as a woman to say. Men, her reason told her, would be shocked. . . . She could write no more.

Virginia Woolf concludes that although men allow themselves great freedom in this respect, they condemn it in women; in her notes for the original speech she added that

> The future of fiction depends very much upon what extent men can be educated to stand free speech in women.

In this essay and throughout her work Virginia Woolf demonstrates an interesting grasp of the psychological aspects of the oppressive conditions in which women were writing. It is clear from her diaries that she was interested in psychoanalysis, and there are many references to this perspective scattered through her writings. In her essay 'The Leaning Tower' Woolf discusses an important difference between the nineteenth-century novelists and her Georgian contemporaries who attempted, as part of a more political approach to writing, to probe themselves more critically:

> By analysing themselves honestly, with help from Dr Freud, these writers have done a great deal to free us from

nineteenth-century suppressions. The writers of the next generation may inherit from them a whole state of mind, a mind no longer crippled, evasive, divided.

This is not to say that Virginia Woolf believed either that psychoanalysis was the clinical cure some claimed it to be, or that the exploration of the unconscious through its insights was the proper object of fiction; in a review of a novel based on an oedipal situation she complained that 'all the characters have become cases'. Yet she was to some extent interested in the development of psychoanalytic theory, was acquainted with many in the British psycho-analytic circle, and visited Freud when he was living in London in 1939 (on which auspicious occasion it is recorded that he gave her a narcissus). In her own novels she was concerned with the exploration of the conscious and the unconscious mind, and also in the relation of states of mind to the public, social relations in which they were embedded. She wrote in *Three Guineas*:

. . . the public and the private worlds are inseparably connected; . . . the tyrannies and servilities of the one are the tyrannies and servilities of the other.

In this respect it might be argued that her ideas were relatively in advance of the general left(ish) Fabian milieu in which she lived and worked. This is perhaps particularly true of her arguments about the position of women. In *Three Guineas* she argues the connection between the political repressiveness of fascism and the exaggeration of divisions between the sexes which have resulted in a concep-tion of man as the protector of woman and thereby led to militarism and belligerence:

The nature of manhood and the nature of womanhood are frequently defined both by Italian and German dictators. Both repeatedly insist that it is the nature of man and

14

indeed the essence of manhood to fight. Hitler, for example, draws a distinction between 'a nation of pacifists and a nation of men'. Both repeatedly insist that it is the nature of womanhood to heal the wounds of the fighter.

Quentin Bell has commented in his biography that Virginia Woolf's friends were silent or critical about this argument, and that his own reaction was that it seemed wrong, at that time, to

> attempt to involve a discussion of women's rights with the far more agonizing and immediate question of what we were to do in order to meet the ever-growing menace of Fascism and war. The connection between the two questions seemed tenuous . . .

Yet to feminists now, and indeed to anyone who has considered Reich's arguments on the sexual repression underlying fascism, the connection is not so tenuous. A recent article on the conception of female sexuality employed in the ideology of fascism[1] has singled out Virginia Woolf as one of the earliest people to perceive the importance of the oppression of women, and the reduction of women to their sexual and reproductive functions, to the fascist programme.

Woolf's attempt to relate the sexual and the political forms part of a wider interest in the relations between public and private aspects of life. The Fabian pacifist milieu in which she existed was one which by and large pre-dated the recognition of the importance of such connections, as is illustrated by a conversation which both Leonard and Virginia Woolf recorded in their diaries. It centred on the argument that socialists should renounce inherited wealth. Virginia Woolf remarked (in her *Diary*, Vol I, 1915–19) that

> psychologically it may be necessary if one is to abolish capitalism

15

whereas Leonard Woolf

> gave us a great many reasons why we should keep what
> we have, and do good work for nothing.

Notwithstanding this, Virginia Woolf concludes that

> I'm one of those who are hampered by the psychological
> hindrance of owning capital.

Clearly Virginia Woolf would have found it impossible to
reconcile the position she took there with the argument of
A Room of One's Own; nonetheless it reveals a perception, however fragmentary and ill-articulated, of the
political nature of personal life. Her general approach to
human relationships was informed by this critical perspective, and can be seen in her novels, particularly in the
treatment of relationships between men and women and
the way in which these are institutionalized in marriage. In
her very earliest novel, *The Voyage Out*, one of the characters comments on the extent to which marriage has, in the
case of the Ambroses, corroded the integrity of their
relationship:

> Even the Ambroses whom he admired and respected
> profoundly – in spite of all the love between them, was
> not their marriage too a compromise? She gave way to
> him; she spoilt him; she arranged things for him; she who
> was all truth to others was not true to her husband, was
> not true to her friends if they came in conflict with her
> husband.

A further point is made in the later novel, *Mrs Dalloway*,
where an explicit connection is drawn between the public
and private aspects of sexual morality and family life, raising
the relationship of bourgeois sexual morality to the institution of prostitution.

Sally suddenly lost her temper, flared up, and told Hugh that he represented all that was most detestable in British middle-class life. She told him that she considered him responsible for the state of 'those poor girls in Piccadilly' – Hugh, the poor gentleman, poor Hugh! – never did a man look more horrified!

We are now familiar with the argument that for women marriage entails financial and therefore emotional dependence, and with the argument that prostitution as an institution protects the bourgeois family, and can perhaps read such passages with more sympathy and recognition than they were accorded in the early part of the century when they were written.

Throughout her work Virginia Woolf consistently argues that the position of women, which is socially and historically determined, has important psychological consequences. She points to the difficulties in overcoming the proscriptions against women's intellectual work, and the obstacles encountered in trying to resist the conventional feminine role. In *A Room of One's Own* she looks back a hundred years, but given her earlier reference to being excluded herself from the library at 'Oxbridge' the point still holds for 1928 when she was writing:

> It would have needed a very stalwart young woman in 1828 to disregard all those snubs and chidings . . . Lock up your libraries if you like; but there is no gate, no lock, no bolt that you can set upon the freedom of my mind.

Virginia Woolf's writings on women and fiction constitute a sustained analysis of the historical determinants of women's literary production. Much as this analysis might gladden the heart of a contemporary Marxist feminist critic, it has, I think, to be examined rather more closely in the light of her work as a whole. In the account of her position given above, I have extracted one line of argument from her work. It is an

17

argument which perhaps has not been sufficiently debated and assessed and, with the exception of recent feminist criticism in the United States,[2] has barely been elicited from her work. Yet the fact cannot be ignored that this argument, although it is central to her theoretical position, is frequently absent from, and even contradicted by, much of her critical work.

This contradiction can be seen in Virginia Woolf's treatment of the Brontës, in ' "Jane Eyre" and "Wuthering Heights" '. There are traces of the familiar dry irony, such as where she comments:

> The drawbacks of being Jane Eyre are not far to seek. Always to be a governess and always to be in love is a serious limitation in a world which is full, after all, of people who are neither one nor the other.

Yet in her consideration of *Wuthering Heights* Virginia Woolf rushes headlong into the conventional romantic mythology of moors, isolation, visions (and it is interesting to note that one of Virginia Woolf's very earliest published articles was the account she gave of a pilgrimage to Haworth in 1904). We find that what Woolf really admires in Emily Brontë's work is its romantic transcendence – its otherworldliness. She writes:

> It is as if she could tear up all that we know human beings by, and fill these unrecognizable transparences with such a gust of life that they transcend reality. Hers, then, is the rarest of all powers. She could free life from its dependence on facts . . .

Where, we may ask, in this, is the critic of *A Room of One's Own*? Is she not precisely arguing here that *Wuthering Heights* is a web spun in mid-air? That it is *not* attached to grossly material things?

We have here an example of Virginia Woolf's view that,

whatever social circumstances may affect the production (or lack of it) of works of art, they have in themselves an almost mystical value. As she put it herself, there are those who prefer the artist to the reformer. This selection of her essays opens with one entitled 'Women and Fiction' in which the contradiction I am discussing is fully revealed. The essay, in some respects of a summary of *A Room of One's Own*, makes two relevant points. Women, she argues, with the change in their social conditions, will in the future be able to perform the office of 'gadfly to the state' hitherto only occupied by men.

> Their novels will deal with social evils and remedies. Their men and women will not be observed wholly in relation to each other emotionally, but as they cohere and clash in groups and classes and races.

Yet then she comments that a second change may take place, and one which is more interesting to those who prefer the butterfly (artist) to the gadfly (reformer):

> They will look beyond the personal and political relationships to the wider questions which the poet tries to solve – of our destiny and the meaning of life.

There can be little doubt that to Virginia Woolf herself, this latter question was the more important. The question that hovers over the head of Lily Briscoe, the artist in *To the Lighthouse*, is 'What is the meaning of life?' and this question was to Virginia Woolf broader and deeper than social or political argument.

Related to this is Virginia Woolf's insistence that the perfect work of art should be unmarred by any intrusion of anger or bitterness. It might be argued that this militates against the feminist analysis discussed earlier. In 'Women and Fiction' she argues that women's writing has suffered in the past from the intrusion of feminist anger. Both

19

George Eliot and Charlotte Brontë suffer from this, in that when we read their works we are conscious of

> someone resenting the treatment of her sex and pleading for its rights. . . . It introduces a distortion and is frequently the cause of weakness.

With lesser women writers, Virginia Woolf argues, the inability to resist this resentment, and the consequent lapse into either 'unnatural self-assertiveness' or 'unnatural docility' is very marked:

> The vision becomes too masculine or it becomes too feminine; it loses its perfect integrity and, with that, its most essential quality as a work of art.

Virginia Woolf, as is well known, argues for androgyny in a work of art. She believed that the writer should not allow an undue consciousness of being of one sex or the other to permeate her or his work. Although in works such as *Three Guineas* she expresses anger and bitterness at the various ways in which women at her time and previously had suffered oppression, she constantly maintains the need, in literature at least, for the artist to stay serene and keep a sense of humour. It may very well be that this primary desire to retain the androgynous integrity of a work of art cuts across the feminist drive in her work. Those of us who have become used to explicit feminist polemic in creative writing may find this difficult to sympathize with, yet this argument remains an important tenet of her criticism. She admires Jane Austen for distancing herself from her own anger:

> When the writer, Jane Austen, wrote down in the most remarkable sketch in the book a little of Lady Greville's conversation, there is no trace of anger at the snub which the clergyman's daughter, Jane Austen, once received.

Similarly Virginia Woolf's account of Elizabeth Barrett Browning's *Aurora Leigh* stresses the need to maintain a properly artistic distance. Although Woolf concedes that the poem 'lives and breathes' and 'we read to the end enthralled', she sees the work as essentially imperfect. In a poem about the development of a woman writer Virginia Woolf is irritated by the fact that

> Mrs Browning could no more conceal herself than she could control herself, a sign no doubt of imperfection in an artist, but a sign also that life has impinged upon art more than life should.

Virginia Woolf's conception of artistic integrity precluded the possibility of an acceptable *explicit* treatment of political questions, including the question of the position of women. In her own novels feminist issues are usually raised in an oblique manner; they arise through conversation, through characterization, and are frequently presented with humour or irony, as for example in the passage from *The Years* where Peggy is talking to a (male) writer at a party:

> Her attention wandered. She had heard it all before, I, I, I – he went on. It was like a vulture's beak pecking, or a vacuum-cleaner sucking, or a telephone bell ringing. I, I, I. But he couldn't help it . . . He could not free himself.
> 'I'm tired,' she apologized. 'I've been up all night,' she explained. 'I'm a doctor –' The fire went out of his face when she said 'I'. That's done it – now he'll go, she thought. He can't be 'you' – he must be 'I'. She smiled. For up he got and off he went.

This passage is an extremely interesting one, and may serve to illustrate the way in which Virginia Woolf presents, with enormous subtlety, some complex points. We may notice that in the assertion of Peggy's own subjective identity, against the egotism of the man, Woolf uses a character who (being a doctor) has escaped from the conventional restrictions of the feminine role. Yet it would be wrong to argue that Virginia Woolf ever subordinated her conception of the integrity of *Art* to the overt expression of her political views, and indeed there is a real tension in her work between these two. While much of her work is explicitly political in nature, and of course *Three Guineas* is highly polemical, she frequently resisted the intrusion of any attitude which, as she wrote to Lytton Strachey, 'gets into the ink and blisters the paper' of her novels. In fact she noted in her diary that *The Years* was 'dangerously near propaganda' and vowed 'I must keep my hands clear'.

Although it is certainly the case that the critical tradition has tended to underestimate Virginia Woolf's feminism, and her interest in material conditions, it also must be said that in retaining the concept of an androgynous art which goes beyond social and political questions Virginia Woolf continually resists the implications of the materialist position she advances in *A Room of One's Own*. This point is perhaps best illustrated by considering the essay 'The Artist and Politics', originally written for the *Daily Worker*, in which she attempts to answer the question as to why, in the 1930s, artists have become interested in politics. Her conclusion, although in passing she has stressed a number of salient points in relation to patronage and the marginal social role of the artist, is ultimately one that confirms the possibility that art, under ideal conditions, may transcend social determination or interference. Ultimately she prefers the romantic voice of the eternal artist to the political voice of the artist as propagandist. The artist, she argues in 'The Artist and Politics', is forced to take part in politics in order to preserve himself and the integrity of his art against the claims of political dogmas which enjoin him to

Celebrate fascism; celebrate communism. Preach what we bid you preach.

Virginia Woolf was herself involved in struggles on behalf of the freedom of the artist. In 1928 she and E. M. Forster wrote to the *Nation* protesting against the banning of Radclyffe Hall's lesbian novel *The Well of Loneliness*. Their letter is characteristically Woolfian:

> The subject-matter of the book exists as a fact among the many other facts of life . . . novelists in England have now been forbidden to mention it by Sir W. Joynson-Hicks. May they mention it incidentally? Although it is forbidden as a main theme, may it be alluded to, or ascribed to subsidiary characters? Perhaps the Home Secretary will issue further orders on this point.

They conclude that a blow has been struck at literature generally, since the production of great literature depends upon 'free minds'. This conclusion, and Virginia Woolf's reiterated argument about 'freedom of mind', is only partially valid. While it is undoubtedly true that material conditions set the boundaries of women's access to literary production it does not by any means follow from this that the removal of external constraints is all that is required for artistic production. Woolf seems to imply what is to us a rather romantic notion of artistic genius – simply establish the correct material and ideological conditions for 'freedom of mind' and the writer is free to create a pure work of art. This view of art was of course far more common in Woolf's time than it is now, when the 'ideology of genius' has been challenged by work on the social context of art. However Woolf's position does raise the interesting question as to whether her general 'materialist' argument could under any circumstances be regarded as a Marxist argument, as some may claim. The answer is surely no. She explores the extent to which, under adverse conditions, art may be restrained and distorted by social conditions, but she retains the notion that in the correct conditions art may be totally divorced from economic, political or ideological constraints.

In her essay 'The Leaning Tower' Virginia Woolf juxtaposes two theories of literature:

> The politician says that a writer is the product of the society in which he lives, as the screw is the product of a screw machine; the artist, that a writer is a heavenly apparition that slides across the sky, grazes the earth, and vanishes.

It is never quite clear from her writings which of these positions she would ultimately subscribe to. The argument of *A Room of One's Own*, exploring the effect of material and ideological conditions on the mind of the writer, seems to verge on the 'politician's' view, yet her ideal of complete freedom of mind reveals a contradictory belief in the transcendence of art. Virginia Woolf, totally committed to the 'integrity' of her art, yet perhaps equally proud, on the publication of *Three Guineas,* of being described by *The Times Literary Supplement* as 'the most brilliant pamphleteer in England', reveals a deep-seated ambivalence as to the rival claims of art and politics. Feminists working in the field of literature today find these problems still unresolved, and perhaps this is why we are still so interested, albeit critically, in her work.

Virginia Woolf on the female literary tradition
It is symptomatic of Virginia Woolf's relevance to contemporary feminism that one of the questions considered in her work on women and fiction – the existence of an intrinsically feminine literary style – is at present highly controversial. The argument that women not only write about different things from men, but that they write about them in a different way, often lies behind feminist literary criticism, and may also underlie the interest in re-examining various female authors of the past. In addition to this some feminists have argued that since men and women are differently constructed as individuals through the learning of language, the

24

relationship of men and women to language is necessarily different. With growing criticism by feminists of the dominance of men in the literary tradition, there has also grown a concern with differences between men and women writers, not only in the images which are used in literature, but in the actual use of language itself. There are times when Virginia Woolf might be thought to subscribe to this view; in her discussion of Jane Austen, in *A Room of One's Own*, she comments on how Austen rejected the classic form of the sentence and created one more suitable for her own use.

> The sentence that was current at the beginning of the nineteenth century ran something like this perhaps:
> 'The grandeur of their works was an argument with them, not to stop short, but to proceed. . . .'
> That is a man's sentence; behind it one can see Johnson, Gibbon, and the rest. It was a sentence that was unsuited to a woman's use. . . . Jane Austen looked at it and laughed at it and devised a perfectly natural, shapely sentence proper for her own use and never departed from it.

Yet this description does not really imply any notion that this use of language is anything other than fully conscious and deliberate; it does not appeal to intrinsic differences between the male and the female author in terms of the language they use. Virginia Woolf's argument is a social, rather than a biological or psychological, one, as is made clearer when she continues:

> There is no reason to think that the form of the epic or of the poetic play suits a woman any more than the sentence suits her. But all the older forms of literature were hardened and set by the time she became a writer. The novel alone was young enough to be soft in her hands – another reason, perhaps, why she wrote novels.

Woolf's position is made even clearer in reviews of Dorothy Richardson's work, a writer who herself claimed in the Foreword to her first book to have created a new, female type of sentence. Virginia Woolf writes

> She has invented, or if she has not invented, developed and applied to her own uses, a sentence which we might call the psychological sentence of the feminine gender. It is of a more elastic fibre than the old, capable of stretching to the extreme, of suspending the frailest particles, of enveloping the vaguest shapes.

The central point which Woolf makes in her review of Dorothy Richardson's novel is that this sentence is not intrinsically a woman's sentence, it is so only by virtue of its subject matter, and the different social experience of women. She continues:

> Other writers of the opposite sex have used sentences of this description and stretched them to the extreme. But there is a difference. Miss Richardson has fashioned her sentence consciously, in order that it may descend to the depths and investigate the crannies of Miriam Henderson's consciousness. It is a woman's sentence, but only in the sense that it is used to describe a woman's mind by a writer who is neither proud nor afraid of anything that she may discover in the psychology of her sex.

In her review of a book on women novelists, Virginia Woolf stresses that it is the subject matter of women's novels which is different from that of men's.

> . . . no one will admit that he can possibly mistake a novel written by a man for a novel written by a woman. There is the obvious and enormous difference of experience in the first place; but the essential difference lies in the fact not

that men describe battles and women the birth of children, but that each sex describes itself. The first words in which either a man or a woman is described are generally enough to determine the sex of the writer . . .

Virginia Woolf's attitude to the question of a 'female language' is particularly interesting in that it informs her response to some of her contemporaries, and her rivals. It is clear that she felt a sense of competition between herself and other women writers of the period, and yet at the same time a curiously sympathetic relationship with their work. Her diary entry on the death of Stella Benson in 1933 explores some of these complex feelings:

> I was walking through Leicester Square . . . just now when I read 'Death of Noted Novelist' on the posters. . . . it is Stella Benson. . . . A very fine steady mind: much suffering; suppressed; – there seems to be some sort of reproach to me in her death, as in K[atherine] M[ansfield]'s. I go on; and they cease. Why? Why not my name on the posters? . . . A curious feeling, when a writer like S.B. dies, that one's response is diminished. . . . My effusion – what I send out – less porous and radiant – as if the thinking stuff were a web that were fertilized only by other people's (her that is) thinking it too: now lacks life.

These feelings can be traced again in the revealing diary entry for 28 November 1919, where Virginia Woolf records her reaction to a highly unfavourable review of *Night and Day* by Katherine Mansfield.

> K.M. wrote a review which irritated me – I thought I saw spite in it. A decorous elderly dullard she described me; Jane Austen up to date. Leonard supposes that she let her wish for my failure have its way with her pen. He could see her looking about for a loophole of escape. 'I'm not

going to call this a success – or if I must, I'll call it the wrong kind of success.'

This reaction to adverse criticism has an interesting consequence:

Today, bearing K.M. in mind, I refused to do Dorothy Richardson for the Supplement. The truth is that when I looked at it, I felt myself looking for faults; hoping for them. And they would have bent my pen, I know. There must be an instinct of self-preservation at work. If she's good then I'm not.

Although Virginia Woolf did not, presumably for the reasons given above, review Richardson's work on this occasion, she did so in the two articles printed in this selection. Dorothy Richardson's admirers, and some other writers, have argued that Virginia Woolf learnt much of her technique from Richardson, who is usually credited as one of the founders of the so-called 'stream of consciousness' method of novel writing. However, the differences between the two writers are highly significant. Richardson's sequence of thirteen semi-autobiographical novels, entitled *Pilgrimage*, relates the story of Miriam Henderson's life solely through the eyes of Miriam herself, and in this respect it differs from the Woolf novels, which employ the technique of constantly shifting from the consciousness of one character to another and of attempting to construct the consciousness of an impersonal narrator. In this respect Virginia Woolf's novels not only avoid the rather suffocating atmosphere of Dorothy Richardson's, but also enable the reader to perceive social life from a variety of perspectives.

Yet what both novelists had in common (a feature not unrelated to their perception of the situation of women), was an emphasis on the consciousness of the individual rather than on some 'realistic' presentation of objective reality. This shared interest in the consciousness of the individual has led to the inevitable charge of triviality. F. R. Leavis, for example, complained in 1942 (in *Scrutiny*) that Virginia Woolf

> seems to shut out all the ranges of experience accompanying those kinds of preoccupation, volitional and moral, with an external world which are not felt primarily as preoccupation with one's consciousness of it.

This comment, containing a grain of truth but no more than this, has set the tone of Virginia Woolf criticism in England for decades. In the light of it what sense can we make of Virginia Woolf's remarks on Dorothy Richardson?

> A man might fall dead at her feet (it is not likely), and Miriam might feel that a violet-coloured ray of light was an important element in her consciousness of the tragedy. If she felt it, she would say it.

Some critics might be justified in regarding this as a strange response from a writer who herself has the reputation of being interested in precisely these minute details of the individual consciousness. Yet there is an important difference between the two, and one which I think Virginia Woolf points to herself in her review of Richardson's *The Tunnel*.

> The method, if triumphant, should make us feel ourselves seated at the centre of another mind, and, according to the artistic gift of the writer, we should perceive in the helter-skelter of flying fragments some unity, significance, or design.

She concludes that with Dorothy Richardson this unity, the resolution of the helter-skelter into a perceptible whole, is not really achieved. The project as a whole never reaches the degree of significance which the reader has hoped for.

Virginia Woolf's own novels, although this is not the place to debate their merits, certainly attempt a far more ambitious degree of significance than Dorothy Richardson's.

Virginia Woolf's complex relationship to Dorothy Richardson's work is complemented by her attitude to Katherine Mansfield, perhaps the other contemporary woman writer who most nearly resembled Virginia Woolf in her literary interests. Again, there is something curious about Woolf's review, printed here, of Katherine Mansfield's diary, which was published after Mansfield's death in 1923 at the age of thirty-four. The phrase 'terribly sensitive' occurs three times in the first two paragraphs, and surely not without a note of implied preciousness – a characteristic all too frequently ascribed by critics to Virginia Woolf herself. It is difficult to read the following without detecting a note of amusement:

> From what point of view is she looking at life, as she sits there, terribly sensitive, registering one after another such diverse impressions?

The juxtaposition of the prosaic 'sits there' with 'terribly sensitive' has a rather unkind effect. Yet Virginia Woolf's attitude to Katherine Mansfield, whom she knew personally, is not properly reflected in this one essay. It is a pity that we have no serious critical essay on her from Virginia Woolf, and it is perhaps legitimate to speculate as to why this is the case. It is clear from her diaries and letters that Virginia Woolf felt a very sincere regard for at least some of Mansfield's work, and her hostility to what she considers to be its failure testifies to an intense interest in the work of potentially her greatest rival. Virginia Woolf, as the following extracts from her diary show, perhaps even felt that she had been deprived, by Katherine Mansfield's early and tragic death, of a worthy rival – and this may account for her unwillingness to capitalize on this, as she would necessarily have done in the writing of a serious critical piece on Mansfield's contribution to literature. On hearing of her death, Virginia Woolf wrote in her diary:

. . . one feels – what? A shock of relief? – a rival the less? Then confusion at feeling so little – then, gradually, blankness and disappointment; then a depression which I could not rouse myself from all that day. When I began to write, it seemed to me there was no point in writing. Katherine won't read it. Katherine's my rival no longer. More generously I felt, but though I can do this better than she could, where is she, who could do what I can't! . . . I think we reached that kind of certainty, in talk about books, or rather about our writings, which I thought had something durable about it. . . . I was jealous of her writing – the only writing I have ever been jealous of. . . . I have the feeling that I shall think of her at intervals all through life. Probably we had something in common which I shall never find in anyone else.

Dorothy Richardson and Katherine Mansfield evoked more interest from Virginia Woolf than other contemporary women writers. She saw them as, like herself, attempting to break significantly with the traditional conventions of literature. In her essay 'Mr Bennett and Mrs Brown', not specifically concerned with women's writing but with the development and changes in fiction generally in the twentieth century, Woolf argued strongly and persuasively for a rejection of the conventions of earlier, descriptive writing. She argued that writers like Galsworthy and Bennett

have given us a house in the hope that we may be able to deduce the human beings who live there.

For contemporary writers, she argued

31

> those conventions are ruin, those tools are death

and she asked the reader, at a time when new literary forms were being tried, to

> tolerate the spasmodic, the obscure, the fragmentary, the failure.

It is not surprising therefore that Virginia Woolf, in her criticism of modern women writers, chose to concentrate on those who were engaged in a similar project to her own of challenging the conventions in literary style and form. Yet when she came to consider the tradition of women's writing as it had developed historically, she demonstrated a perception of these writers which was grounded in a historical appreciation of their work. She did not judge them by the standards she applied to the writers of her own age, but judged them according to what she considered to be their contribution to literature at the time in which they were writing. It must be stressed that although Virginia Woolf distanced herself as a writer from previous women novelists, for example, noting in her diary that

> I had rather write in my own way of 'four Passionate Snails' than be, as K.M. maintains, Jane Austen over again.

she nevertheless was deeply conscious of a tradition of female writing in which she was immersed. As is clear from *A Room of One's Own* and elsewhere, she had a great interest not only in the lives of earlier women writers, but in the social and historical development of the role of the woman writer. In addition to this, there are numerous essays on individual women which appear regularly in her collected essays. Pioneers of women's education, 'eccentrics', women involved in politics – all these and more appear as the subjects of her essays. Frequently these pieces were prompted by reading and reviewing biographies, collections of letters and memoirs, and they testify to an abiding interest in the lives of women at different stages of (predominantly English) history. Only connected with the question of women and literature to the extent that the biographies were frequently written by women, the letters edited by women and so on, they do not properly form part of the essays printed here, but are in themselves an interesting aspect of Virginia Woolf's feminist work.

It is Virginia Woolf's concern with the tradition of women writers, and her insistence that their work be viewed in its historical context, that has determined the arrangement of the essays in the second part of the present selection. They are laid out here in the chronological order of the subjects about whom she was writing, beginning with the Duchess of Newcastle (1624–74) and ending with Dorothy Richardson, who died in 1957. We should note, however, that Virginia Woolf was not engaged in a project simply to resurrect forgotten women writers. She maintained a thoroughly critical attitude to their work, and was not inclined to subordinate what she considered to be aesthetic judgements to a desire to create a canon of women's writing. The essay 'A Scribbling Dame' has been included to illustrate this point. She concludes not only that Eliza Haywood was an extremely indifferent writer, but that the resources of Columbia University have been wasted upon the exercise of cataloguing her work and drawing it to the attention of a reading public who could profitably spend their time in other ways. Although a rather uncharitable review, the essay does draw our attention to the dangers of adopting an uncritical view of women's literary production. The development of literary critical theory since Virginia Woolf's day has quite properly challenged the ease with which throughout her work she presumed to state, as did all other critics, confident aesthetic judgements about the quality or rank of a work of art. It would, however, be wrong to reduce Virginia Woolf's criticism to this process of

'league-tabling' of writers, for she consistently raises issues
– social, political, historical – which can be separated from
these aesthetic considerations. (It might well also be added,
that to present readers – caught up in an almost total confusion on the subject of aesthetic value – her judgements
have a refreshing conviction about them which is rather
appealing.)

It is a measure of Virginia Woolf's interest in the question
of a female literary tradition, and of her insistence on the
importance of the historical context in which writers produce their work, that she speculated upon the future
developments she and others would see. To return to the
essay 'Professions for Women', we can note again her
remarks on the difficulties she encountered in speaking
frankly about sexuality. This problem – 'telling the truth
about my own experiences as a body' – proved intractable.
'I do not think I solved it' she admitted, and added that 'I
doubt that any woman has solved it yet.' In the future,
however, this might be possible, if men could be persuaded
to 'stand free speech in women'. A related point is made in
the closing section of *A Room of One's Own* where Virginia
Woolf alludes to her earlier remark that women, in literature
written by men, are almost invariably portrayed as they
relate to men and not as they relate to each other and to their
own work. She is heartened to read the work of one of her
fictitious contemporaries, a younger woman whom she
names Mary Carmichael. In this novel, she notes, two
women are presented in the laboratory where they worked
and it is recorded that 'Chloe liked Olivia'. She goes on to
comment that

> Now if Chloe likes Olivia and they share a laboratory,
> which of itself will make their friendship more varied and
> lasting because it will be less personal; if Mary Carmichael
> knows how to write . . . if she has a room to herself . . . if
> she has five hundred a year of her own . . . then I think
> that something of great importance has happened.

For if Chloe likes Olivia and Mary Carmichael knows how to express it she will light a torch in that vast chamber where nobody has yet been.

Virginia Woolf concludes her reading of Mary Carmichael's novel with the comment 'Give her another hundred years . . . and she will write a better book . . .', on the assumption that the conditions in which women write will improve in that period.

Virginia Woolf wrote *A Room of One's Own* fifty years ago. The Home Office does not now ban lesbian novels; women now have formally greater equality of access to education than they did in 1929; women are beginning to control the publication and distribution of their work; some women may indeed possess 'a room of their own' and considerably more than £500 a year. Yet these 'outward' changes, which are limited in character, do not necessarily bring with them corresponding changes in attitudes, prejudice, ideology. As Virginia Woolf wrote:

> It will be a long time still, I think, before a woman can sit down to write a book without finding a phantom to be slain, a rock to be dashed against. And if this is so in literature, the freest of all professions for women, how is it in the new professions which you are for the first time entering?

Fifty years later we may want to disagree with some of her emphases. Outwardly, we can argue cogently, there *are* obstacles for women which men do not face; indeed we know from *Three Guineas* that Virginia Woolf was herself only too well aware of them. We could suggest that there are fewer obstacles in the professions, with which she was concerned, than exist for the majority of working women. It is easy for us to make these qualifications, just as it is easy for us to identify contradictions and dilemmas in Virginia Woolf's arguments. They do not, however, alter the fact

35

that Virginia Woolf's critical essays offer us an unparalleled account of the development of women's writing, perceptive discussion of her predecessors and contemporaries, and a pertinent insistence on the material conditions which have structured women's consciousness.

Notes
1. Maria-Antonietta Macciocchi, in her discussion of 'Female Sexuality in Fascist Ideology' (*Feminist Review*, 1979, No 1), cites Virginia Woolf as one of the earliest people to recognize the connection between the political repression of fascism and the sexual oppression of women.
2. See for example Jane Marcus, ' "No more horses": Virginia Woolf on art and propaganda', *Women's Studies*, 1977, Vol 4, pp 265–90; Sallie Sears, 'Notes on Sexuality: *The Years* and *Three Guineas*', Bulletin of the New York Public Library, 1977, Vol 80, pp 211–20; Berenice A. Carroll, ' "To Crush Him In Our Own Country": The Political Thought of Virginia Woolf', *Feminist Studies*, 1978, Vol 4, No 1; Jane Marcus 'Art and Anger', *Feminist Studies*, 1978, Vol 4, No 1. In this last-mentioned paper Marcus argues that '. . . it was anger that impelled her art and intellect that combed out the snarls . . .' and concludes that 'Anger is *not* anathema in art; it is a primary source of creative energy.' This view, although correctly stressing the political force of Woolf's work as a whole, does not, I think, take account of Woolf's explicitly stated desire to avoid propaganda in her novels.

Virginia Woolf sources
Essays by Virginia Woolf referred to in this Introduction and not included in this selection can be found as follows:
'The Leaning Tower' and 'The Artist and Politics' in *The Moment and Other Essays* (1947); 'Mr Bennett and Mrs Brown' in *The Captain's Death Bed and Other Essays*

(1950); 'On Not Knowing Greek' in *The Common Reader*: First Series (1925).

Virginia Woolf's *Diary*, edited by Anne Olivier Bell, is in course of publication in five volumes (1977–81).

A Writer's Diary (extracts from Virginia Woolf's *Diary*, edited by Leonard Woolf) was published in 1953.

The unrevised text of the speech given to the London/National Society for Women's Service in 1931, which forms the basis for Woolf's essay 'Professions for Women', is published in *The Pargiters* (edited by Mitchell A. Leaska) (1978).

Virginia Woolf's *Letters*, edited by Nigel Nicolson and Joanne Trautmann, are in course of publication in six volumes (1975–80).

The authorized *Biography* of Virginia Woolf, by Quentin Bell, is published in two volumes: Vol I Virginia Stephen 1882–1912; Vol II Mrs Woolf 1912–1941 (1972).

All the above works are published by The Hogarth Press, as are Virginia Woolf's novels and non-fiction, including *A Room of One's Own* and *Three Guineas*. Much of her work has subsequently been reprinted in various paperback editions.

Virginia Woolf's less accessible publications can be traced by consulting B. J. Kirkpatrick's comprehensive *Bibliography of Virginia Woolf* (Revised edition, Oxford University Press, 1967).

Virginia Woolf published in her lifetime two books of critical essays, *The Common Reader*: First Series (1925), Second Series (1932). After her death several further volumes were published under the following titles:

The Death of the Moth (1942); *The Moment and Other Essays* (1947); *The Captain's Deathbed and Other Essays* (1950); *Granite and Rainbow* (1958); *Contemporary Writers* (1965); *Books and Portraits* (1977).

In 1966 and 1967 Leonard Woolf published four volumes of *Collected Essays* by Virginia Woolf, drawn from the volumes listed above. To avoid confusion the notes which introduce the essays in this selection refer only to the titled volumes and not to the *Collected Essays*.

Further reading
It would be futile to attempt to provide a guide through the vast critical literature on Virginia Woolf. A good indication of its range can be obtained from Majumdar, Robin and McLaurin, Allen (eds) *Virginia Woolf: The Critical Heritage* (Routledge and Kegan Paul, London, 1975). One work stands out above the rest in its brilliant assessment of Woolf's place in the development of western literature: Erich Auerbach's chapter on *To the Lighthouse* in his study *Mimesis: The Representation of Reality in Western Literature* (Princeton University Press, New Jersey, 1968).

Feminist criticism of Woolf begins with Winifred Holtby's *Virginia Woolf* (Wishart, London, 1932). Kate Millett, in her *Sexual Politics* (reprinted by Virago, London, 1978) attacks Woolf for having allegedly 'glorified two housewives, Mrs Ramsay and Mrs Dalloway', and Elaine Showalter regards Woolf's 'flight into androgyny' as a disastrous influence on feminist writing (*A Literature of Their Own: British Women Novelists From Brontë to Lessing*, Chapter X, Virago, London, 1978). Several writers have attempted to read Woolf's work in the light of a supposed opposition between its 'masculine' and 'feminine' qualities: Herbert Marder's *Feminism and Art: A Study of Virginia Woolf*, University of Chicago Press, 1968; Nancy Topping Bazin's *Virginia Woolf and the Androgynous Vision*, Rutgers University Press, 1973; James Naremore's *The World Without a Self: Virginia Woolf and the Novel*, Yale University Press, 1973; and Alice Van Buren Kelley's *The Novels of Virginia Woolf: Fact and Vision*, University of Chicago Press, 1973, tend to work with this assumption. There are useful discussions of Woolf in Carolyn Heilbrun's *Towards Androgyny*, Gollancz, 1973, and Sydney Janet Kaplan's *Feminine Consciousness in the Modern British Novel*,

Illinois University Press, 1975. Feminists will be interested in Aileen Pippett's *The Moth and the Star* (Little Brown Co Inc, Boston, 1975), a biography of Virginia Woolf based on her correspondence with Victoria Sackville-West. Developments in Woolf criticism in the United States can be followed through the *Virginia Woolf Miscellany* (Department of English, Sonoma State College, Rohnert Park, California). See also the references listed in Note 2 above.

Acknowledgements
My deepest thanks go to Stephanie Dowrick of The Women's Press, who not only conceived this book but worked diligently to ensure its final appearance. I am also particularly indebted to Jean Radford, with whom I have collaborated on a paper on Virginia Woolf and Dorothy Richardson, and to Quentin and Olivier Bell for their help in realizing this project. I am grateful to Cora Kaplan, Mary McIntosh, Julia Naish, William Outhwaite, Marion Shaw and Helen Taylor for their comments on an earlier draft of the Introduction.

PART ONE

Women and Fiction

This essay appeared in *The Forum*, March 1929, and is reprinted in *Granite and Rainbow*.

The title of this article can be read in two ways: it may allude to women and the fiction that they write, or to women and the fiction that is written about them. The ambiguity is intentional, for in dealing with women as writers, as much elasticity as possible is desirable; it is necessary to leave oneself room to deal with other things besides their work, so much has that work been influenced by conditions that have nothing whatever to do with art.

The most superficial inquiry into women's writing instantly raises a host of questions. Why, we ask at once, was there no continuous writing done by women before the eighteenth century? Why did they then write almost as habitually as men, and in the course of that writing produce, one after another, some of the classics of English fiction? And why did their art then, and why to some extent does their art still, take the form of fiction?

A little thought will show us that we are asking questions to which we shall get, as answer, only further fiction. The answer lies at present locked in old diaries, stuffed away in old drawers, half-obliterated in the memories of the aged. It is to be found in the lives of the obscure – in those almost unlit corridors of history where the figures of generations of women are so dimly, so fitfully perceived. For very little is known about women. The history of England is the history of the male line, not of the female. Of our fathers we know always some fact, some distinction. They were soldiers or they were sailors; they filled that office or they made that law. But of our mothers, our grandmothers, our great-grandmothers, what remains? Nothing but a tradition. One was beautiful; one was red-haired; one was kissed by a Queen. We know nothing of them except their names and the dates of their marriages and the number of children they bore.

Thus, if we wish to know why at any particular time women did this or that, why they wrote nothing, why on the other hand they wrote masterpieces, it is extremely difficult to tell. Anyone who should seek among those old papers, who should turn history wrong side out and so construct a faithful picture of the daily life of the ordinary women in Shakespeare's time, in Milton's time, in Johnson's time, would not only write a book of astonishing interest, but would furnish the critic with a weapon which he now lacks. The extraordinary woman depends on the ordinary woman. It is only when we know what were the conditions of the average woman's life – the number of her children, whether she had money of her own, if she had a room to herself, whether she had help in bringing up her family, if she had servants, whether part of the housework was her task – it is only when we can measure the way of life and the experience of life made possible to the ordinary woman that we can account for the success or failure of the extraordinary woman as a writer.

Strange spaces of silence seem to separate one period of activity from another. There was Sappho and a little group of women all writing poetry on a Greek island six hundred years before the birth of Christ. They fall silent. Then about the year 1000 we find a certain court lady, the Lady Murasaki, writing a very long and beautiful novel in Japan. But in England in the sixteenth century, when the dramatists and poets were most active, the women were dumb. Elizabethan literature is exclusively masculine. Then, at the end of the eighteenth century and in the beginning of the nineteenth, we find women again writing – this time in England – with extraordinary frequency and success.

Law and custom were of course largely responsible for these strange intermissions of silence and speech. When a woman was liable, as she was in the fifteenth century, to be beaten and flung about the room if she did not marry the man of her parents' choice, the spiritual atmosphere was not favourable to the production of works of art. When she was married without her own consent to a man who thereupon became her lord and master, 'so far at least as law and custom could make him', as she was in the time of the Stuarts, it is likely she had little time for writing, and less encouragement. The immense effect of environment and suggestion upon the mind, we in our psychoanalytical age are beginning to realize. Again, with memoirs and letters to help us, we are beginning to understand how abnormal is the effort needed to produce a work of art, and what shelter and what support the mind of the artist requires. Of those facts the lives and letters of men like Keats and Carlyle and Flaubert assure us.

Thus it is clear that the extraordinary outburst of fiction in the beginning of the nineteenth century in England was heralded by innumerable slight changes in law and customs and manners. And women of the nineteenth century had some leisure; they had some education. It was no longer the exception for women of the middle and upper classes to choose their own husbands. And it is significant that of the four great women novelists – Jane Austen, Emily Brontë, Charlotte Brontë, and George Eliot – not one had a child, and two were unmarried.

Yet, though it is clear that the ban upon writing had been removed, there was still, it would seem, considerable pressure upon women to write novels. No four women can have been more unlike in genius and character than these four. Jane Austen can have had nothing in common with George Eliot; George Eliot was the direct opposite of Emily Brontë. Yet all were trained for the same profession; all, when they wrote, wrote novels.

Fiction was, as fiction still is, the easiest thing for a woman to write. Nor is it difficult to find the reason. A novel is the least concentrated form of art. A novel can be taken up or put down more easily than a play or a poem. George Eliot left her work to nurse her father. Charlotte Brontë put down her pen to pick the eyes out of the potatoes. And living as she did in the common sitting-room, surrounded by people, a woman was trained to use her mind in observation and upon the analysis of character. She was trained to be a novelist and not to be a poet.

Even in the nineteenth century, a woman lived almost solely in her home and her emotions. And those ninteenth-century novels, remarkable as they were, were profoundly influenced by the fact that the women who wrote them were excluded by their sex from certain kinds of experience. That experience has a great influence upon fiction is indisputable. The best part of Conrad's novels, for instance, would be destroyed if it had been impossible for him to be a sailor. Take away all that Tolstoi knew of war as a soldier, of life and society as a rich young man whose education admitted him to all sorts of experience, and *War and Peace* would be incredibly impoverished.

Yet *Pride and Prejudice*, *Wuthering Heights*, *Villette*, and *Middlemarch* were written by women from whom was forcibly withheld all experience save that which could be met with in a middle-class drawing–room. No first-hand experience of war or seafaring or politics or business was possible for them. Even their emotional life was strictly regulated by law and custom. When George Eliot ventured to live with Mr Lewes without being his wife, public opinion was scandalized. Under its pressure she withdrew into a suburban seclusion which, inevitably, had the worst possible effects upon her work. She wrote that unless people asked of their own accord to come and see her, she never invited them. At the same time, on the other side of Europe, Tolstoi was living a free life as a soldier, with men and women of all classes, for which nobody censured him and from which his novels drew much of their astonishing breadth and vigour.

But the novels of women were not affected only by the necessarily narrow range of the writer's experience. They showed, at least in the nineteenth century, another characteristic which may be traced to the writer's sex. In *Middlemarch* and in *Jane Eyre* we are conscious not merely of the writer's character, as we are conscious of the character of Charles Dickens, but we are conscious of a woman's presence – of someone resenting the treatment of her sex and pleading for its rights. This brings into women's writing an element which is entirely absent from a man's, unless, indeed, he happens to be a working-man, a Negro, or one who for some other reason is conscious of disability. It introduces a distortion and is frequently the cause of weakness. The desire to plead some personal cause or to make a character the mouthpiece of some personal discontent or grievance always has a distressing effect, as if the spot at which the reader's attention is directed were suddenly twofold instead of single.

The genius of Jane Austen and Emily Brontë is never more convincing than in their power to ignore such claims and solicitations and to hold on their way unperturbed by scorn or censure. But it needed a very serene or a very powerful mind to resist the temptation to anger. The ridicule, the censure, the assurance of inferiority in one form or another which were lavished upon women who practised an art, provoked such reactions naturally enough. One sees the effect in Charlotte Brontë's indignation, in

George Eliot's resignation. Again and again one finds it in the work of the lesser women writers – in their choice of a subject, in their unnatural self-assertiveness, in their unnatural docility. Moreover, insincerity leaks in almost unconsciously. They adopt a view in deference to authority. The vision becomes too masculine or it becomes too feminine; it loses its perfect integrity and, with that, its most essential quality as a work of art.

The great change that has crept into women's writing is, it would seem, a change of attitude. The woman writer is no longer bitter. She is no longer angry. She is no longer pleading and protesting as she writes. We are approaching, if we have not yet reached, the time when her writing will have little or no foreign influence to disturb it. She will be able to concentrate upon her vision without distraction from outside. The aloofness that was once within the reach of genius and originality is only now coming within reach of ordinary women. Therefore the average novel by a woman is far more genuine and far more interesting today than it was a hundred or even fifty years ago.

But it is still true that before a woman can write exactly as she wishes to write, she has many difficulties to face. To begin with, there is the technical difficulty – so simple, apparently; in reality, so baffling – that the very form of the sentence does not fit her. It is a sentence made by men; it is too loose, too heavy, too pompous for a woman's use. Yet in a novel, which covers so wide a stretch of ground, an ordinary and usual type of sentence has to be found to carry the reader on easily and naturally from one end of the book to the other. And this a woman must make for herself, altering and adapting the current sentence until she writes one that takes the natural shape of her thought without crushing or distorting it.

But that, after all, is only a means to an end, and the end is still to be reached only when a woman has the courage to surmount opposition and the determination to be true to herself. For a novel, after all, is a statement about a thousand different objects – human, natural, divine; it is an attempt to relate them to each other. In every novel of merit these different elements are held in place by the force of the writer's vision. But they have another order also, which is the order imposed upon them by convention. And as men are the arbiters of that convention, as they have established an order of values in life, so too, since fiction is largely based on life, these values prevail there also to a very great extent.

It is probable, however, that both in life and in art the values of a woman are not the values of a man. Thus, when a woman comes to write a novel, she will find that she is perpetually wishing to alter the established values – to make serious what appears insignificant to a man, and trivial what is to him important. And for that, of course, she will be criticized; for the critic of the opposite sex will be genuinely puzzled and surprised by an attempt to alter the current scale of values, and will see in it not merely a difference of view, but a view that is weak, or trivial, or sentimental, because it differs from his own.

But here, too, women are coming to be more independent of opinion. They are beginning to respect their own sense of values. And for this reason the subject matter of their novels begins to show certain changes. They are less interested, it would seem, in themselves; on the other hand, they are more interested in other women. In the early nineteenth century, women's novels were largely autobiographical. One of the motives that led them to write was the desire to expose their own suffering, to plead their own cause. Now that this desire is no longer so urgent, women are beginning to explore their own sex, to write of women as women have never been written of before; for of course, until very lately, women in literature were the creation of men.

Here again there are difficulties to overcome, for, if one may generalize, not only do women submit less readily to observation than men, but their lives are far less tested and examined by the ordinary processes of life. Often nothing tangible remains of a woman's day. The food that has been

49

cooked is eaten; the children that have been nursed have gone out into the world. Where does the accent fall? What is the salient point for the novelist to seize upon? It is difficult to say. Her life has an anonymous character which is baffling and puzzling in the extreme. For the first time, this dark country is beginning to be explored in fiction; and at the same moment a woman has also to record the changes in women's minds and habits which the opening of the professions has introduced. She has to observe how their lives are ceasing to run underground; she has to discover what new colours and shadows are showing in them now that they are exposed to the outer world.

If, then, one should try to sum up the character of women's fiction at the present moment, one would say that it is courageous; it is sincere; it keeps closely to what women feel. It is not bitter. It does not insist upon its femininity. But at the same time, a woman's book is not written as a man would write it. These qualities are much commoner than they were, and they give even to second- and third-rate work the value of truth and the interest of sincerity.

But in addition to these good qualities, there are two that call for a word more of discussion. The change which has turned the English woman from a nondescript influence, fluctuating and vague, to a voter, a wage-earner, a responsible citizen, has given her both in her life and in her art a turn towards the impersonal. Her relations now are not only emotional; they are intellectual, they are political. The old system which condemned her to squint askance at things through the eyes or through the interests of husband or brother, has given place to the direct and practical interests of one who must act for herself, and not merely influence the acts of others. Hence her attention is being directed away from the personal centre which engaged it exclusively in the past to the impersonal, and her novels naturally become more critical of society, and less analytical of individual lives.

We may expect that the office of gadfly to the state, which has been so far a male prerogative, will now be discharged by women also. Their novels will deal with social evils and remedies. Their men and women will not be observed wholly in relation to each other emotionally, but as they cohere and clash in groups and classes and races. That is one change of some importance. But there is another more interesting to those who prefer the butterfly to the gadfly – that is to say, the artist to the reformer. The greater impersonality of women's lives will encourage the poetic spirit, and it is in poetry that women's fiction is still weakest. It will lead them to be less absorbed in facts and no longer content to record with astonishing acuteness the minute details which fall under their own observation. They will look beyond the personal and political relationships to the wider questions which the poet tries to solve – of our destiny and the meaning of life.

The basis of the poetic attitude is of course largely founded upon material things. It depends upon leisure, and a little money, and the chance which money and leisure give to observe impersonally and dispassionately. With money and leisure at their service, women will naturally occupy themselves more than has hitherto been possible with the craft of letters. They will make a fuller and a more subtle use of the instrument of writing. Their technique will become bolder and richer.

In the past, the virtue of women's writing often lay in its divine spontaneity, like that of the blackbird's song or the thrush's. It was untaught; it was from the heart. But it was also, and much more often, chattering and garrulous – mere talk spilt over paper and left to dry in pools and blots. In future, granted time and books and a little space in the house for herself, literature will become for women, as for men, an art to be studied. Women's gift will be trained and strengthened. The novel will cease to be the dumping-ground for the personal emotions. It will become, more than at present, a work of art like any other, and its resources and its limitations will be explored.

From this it is a short step to the practice of the sophisti-cated arts, hitherto so little practised by women – to the

51

writing of essays and criticism, of history and biography. And that, too, if we are considering the novel, will be of advantage; for besides improving the quality of the novel itself, it will draw off the aliens who have been attracted to fiction by its accessibility while their hearts lay elsewhere. Thus will the novel be rid of those excrescences of history and fact which, in our time, have made it so shapeless.

So, if we may prophesy, women in time to come will write fewer novels, but better novels; and not novels only, but poetry and criticism and history. But in this, to be sure, one is looking ahead to that golden, that perhaps fabulous, age when women will have what has so long been denied them – leisure, and money, and a room to themselves.

Women and Leisure

The *Nation and Athenaeum* carried a review of Virginia Woolf's *A Room of One's Own*, by Lyn Ll. Irvine, on 9 November 1929. This reply by Virginia Woolf was published on 16 November.

SIR, – I must thank Miss Irvine for her very intelligent and generous article on my book, *A Room of One's Own*. But perhaps you will allow me to dispute one or two of her contentions. 'The poorest community of men,' she says, 'would never sit down week in, week out, to such a diet' (i.e., a diet of prunes and custard). And she infers that men are therefore endowed with some desirable power that women lack. But, after all, the majority of Englishmen are sitting down at this moment to such a diet. The working-class man does not possess either £500 a year or a room of his own. And if the majority of men, without the burden of child-bearing and with the professions open to them, yet find it impossible to earn a wage that admits of leisure and the production of works of art, it would seem to prove that both sexes, men as well as women, are forced to eat prunes and custard not because they like them, or are patient or can imagine nothing better, but because that is all that they can get. It is the middle-class man to whom we owe our art; but whether he would have enjoyed his very valuable degree of comfort and prosperity had the duty of child-birth been laid upon him in the flower of his youth, and had all the professions been closed to him by his sex, seems to me disputable.

Then again, Miss Irvine contends that if the Brontë sisters had lived now they would have become schoolmistresses, and would have travelled abroad under the auspices of Thomas Cook and Son; but they would have lost their leisure, she says, and we should have lost *Jane Eyre* and *Wuthering Heights*. What kind of 'leisure' the women of the nineteenth century enjoyed is, I think, made very plain by Florence Nightingale in *Cassandra*. 'Women never have half an hour in all their lives (excepting before or after anybody is up in the house) that they can call their own, without fear of offending or of hurting someone.' I submit that Charlotte Brontë would have enjoyed more true leisure as a schoolmistress now than she did as the daughter at home in close attendance upon a beloved, but it would seem somewhat exacting, parent in a vicarage in a graveyard. Nor can I stifle my suspicion that if Emily had travelled in the summer holidays even under the guidance of Mr Cook she might not have died of consumption at the age of twenty-nine. But, of course, in no circumstances could the Brontë sisters have been either typical schoolmistresses or typical globe-trotters. They remain rare and remarkable women. And my argument was that if we wish to increase the supply of rare and remarkable women like the Brontës we should give the Joneses and the Smiths rooms of their own and five hundred a year. One cannot grow fine flowers in a thin soil. And hitherto the soil – I mean no disrespect to Miss Smith and Miss Jones – has been very starved and very stony. – Yours, &c.,

VIRGINIA WOOLF.

The Intellectual Status of Women

The *New Statesman* of 2 October 1920 carried a discussion by their columnist 'Affable Hawk' (alias Desmond MacCarthy) of Arnold Bennett's *Our Women* and Orlo William's *The Good Englishman*. 'Affable Hawk' endorsed Bennett's view that 'women are inferior to men in intellectual power' and thereby provoked this letter from Virginia Woolf, which was published on 9 October. It is reprinted, with a summary of 'Affable Hawk's response, and the text of Virginia Woolf's subsequent letter, in Appendix III of her *Diary*, Vol 2 (ed Anne Olivier Bell, 1978).

SIR, – Like most women, I am unable to face the depression and the loss of self-respect which Mr Arnold Bennett's blame and Mr Orlo Williams' praise – if it is not the other way about – would certainly cause me if I read their books in the bulk. I taste them, therefore, in sips at the hands of reviewers. But I cannot swallow the teaspoonful administered in your columns last week by Affable Hawk. The fact that women are inferior to men in intellectual power, he says, 'stares him in the face'. He goes on to agree with Mr Bennett's conclusion that 'no amount of education and liberty of action will sensibly alter it'. How, then, does Affable Hawk account for the fact which stares me, and I should have thought any other impartial observer, in the face, that the seventeenth century produced more remarkable women that the sixteenth, the eighteenth than the seventeenth, and the nineteenth than all three put together? When I compare the Duchess of Newcastle with Jane Austen, the matchless Orinda with Emily Brontë, Mrs

Haywood with George Eliot, Aphra Behn with Charlotte Brontë, Jane Grey with Jane Harrison, the advance in intellectual power seems to me not only sensible but immense; the comparison with men not in the least one that inclines me to suicide; and the effects of education and liberty scarcely to be overrated. In short, though pessimism about the other sex is always delightful and invigorating, it seems a little sanguine of Mr Bennett and Affable Hawk to indulge in it with such certainty on the evidence before them. Thus, though women have every reason to hope that the intellect of the male sex is steadily diminishing, it would be unwise, until they have more evidence than the great war and the great peace supply, to announce it as a fact. In conclusion, if Affable Hawk sincerely wishes to discover a great poetess, why does he let himself be fobbed off with a possible authoress of the Odyssey? Naturally, I cannot claim to know Greek as Mr Bennett and Affable Hawk know it, but I have often been told that Sappho was a woman, and that Plato and Aristotle placed her with Homer and Archilocus among the greatest of their poets. That Mr Bennett can name fifty of the male sex who are indisputably her superiors is therefore a welcome surprise, and if he will publish their names I will promise, as an act of that submission which is so dear to my sex, not only to buy their works but, so far as my faculties allow, to learn them by heart. – Yours, etc.

VIRGINIA WOOLF.

Professions for Women

This essay is published in *The Death of the Moth*. It is based on a speech given to the London/ National Society for Women's Service on 21 January 1931. The typescript of this speech, which is about three times the length of the essay, is reproduced (including cancelled passages and alternative wordings) in *The Pargiters*, edited by Mitchell A. Leaska, 1978.

When your secretary invited me to come here, she told me that your Society is concerned with the employment of women and she suggested that I might tell you something about my own professional experiences. It is true I am a woman; it is true I am employed; but what professional experiences have I had? It is difficult to say. My profession is literature; and in that profession there are fewer experiences for women than in any other, with the exception of the stage – fewer, I mean, that are peculiar to women. For the road was cut many years ago – by Fanny Burney, by Aphra Behn, by Harriet Martineau, by Jane Austen, by George Eliot – many famous women, and many more unknown and forgotten, have been before me, making the path smooth, and regulating my steps. Thus, when I came to write, there were very few material obstacles in my way. Writing was a reputable and harmless occupation. The family peace was not broken by the scratching of a pen. No demand was made upon the family purse. For ten and sixpence one can buy paper enough to write all the plays of Shakespeare – if one has a mind that way. Pianos and models, Paris, Vienna and Berlin, masters and mistresses, are not needed by a writer. The cheapness of writing paper is, of course, the reason why women have succeeded as writers before they have succeeded in the other professions.

But to tell you my story – it is a simple one. You have only got to figure to yourselves a girl in a bedroom with a pen in her hand. She had only to move that pen from left to right – from ten o'clock to one. Then it occurred to her to do what is simple and cheap enough after all – to slip a few of those pages into an envelope, fix a penny stamp in the corner, and drop the envelope into the red box at the corner. It was thus that I became a journalist; and my effort was rewarded on the first day of the following month – a very glorious day it was for me – by a letter from an editor containing a cheque for one pound ten shillings and sixpence. But to show you how little I deserve to be called a professional woman, how little I know of the struggles and difficulties of such lives, I have to admit that instead of spending that sum upon bread and butter, rent, shoes and stockings, or butcher's bills, I went out and bought a cat – a beautiful cat, a Persian cat, which very soon involved me in bitter disputes with my neighbours.

What could be easier than to write articles and to buy Persian cats with the profits? But wait a moment. Articles have to be about something. Mine, I seem to remember, was about a novel by a famous man. And while I was writing this review, I discovered that if I were going to review books I should need to do battle with a certain phantom. And the phantom was a woman, and when I came to know her better I called her after the heroine of a famous poem, The Angel in the House. It was she who used to come between me and my paper when I was writing reviews. It was she who bothered me and wasted my time and so tormented me that at last I killed her. You who come of a younger and happier generation

58

may not have heard of her – you may not know what I mean by the Angel in the House. I will describe her as shortly as I can. She was intensely sympathetic. She was immensely charming. She was utterly unselfish. She excelled in the difficult arts of family life. She sacrificed herself daily. If there was chicken, she took the leg; if there was a draught she sat in it – in short she was so constituted that she never had a mind or a wish of her own, but preferred to sympathize always with the minds and wishes of others. Above all – I need not say it – she was pure. Her purity was supposed to be her chief beauty – her blushes, her great grace. In those days – the last of Queen Victoria – every house had its Angel. And when I came to write I encountered her with the very first words. The shadow of her wings fell on my page; I heard the rustling of her skirts in the room. Directly, that is to say, I took my pen in my hand to review that novel by a famous man, she slipped behind me and whispered: 'My dear, you are a young woman. You are writing about a book that has been written by a man. Be sympathetic; be tender; flatter; deceive; use all the arts and wiles of our sex. Never let anybody guess that you have a mind of your own. Above all, be pure.' And she made as if to guide my pen. I now record the one act for which I take some credit to myself, though the credit rightly belongs to some excellent ancestors of mine who left me a certain sum of money – shall we say five hundred pounds a year? – so that it was not necessary for me to depend solely on charm for my living. I turned upon her and caught her by the throat. I did my best to kill her. My excuse, if I were to be had up in a court of law, would be that I acted in self-defence. Had I not killed her she would have killed me. She would have plucked the heart out of my writing. For, as I found, directly I put pen to paper, you cannot review even a novel without having a mind of your own, without expressing what you think to be the truth about human relations, morality, sex. And all these questions, according to the Angel of the House, cannot be dealt with freely and openly by women; they must charm, they must conciliate, they must – to put it bluntly – tell lies if they are to succeed. Thus, whenever I felt the shadow of her wing or the radiance of her halo upon my page, I took up the inkpot and flung it at her. She died hard. Her fictitious nature was of great assistance to her. It is far harder to kill a phantom than a reality. She was always creeping back when I thought I had despatched her. Though I flatter myself that I killed her in the end, the struggle was severe; it took much time that had better have been spent upon learning Greek grammar; or in roaming the world in search of adventures. But it was a real experience; it was an experience that was found to befall all women writers at that time. Killing the Angel in the House was part of the occupation of a woman writer.

But to continue my story. The Angel was dead; what then remained? You may say that what remained was a simple and common object – a young woman in a bedroom with an inkpot. In other words, now that she had rid herself of falsehood, that young woman had only to be herself. Ah, but what is 'herself'? I mean, what is a woman? I assure you, I do not know. I do not believe that you know. I do not believe that anybody can know until she has expressed herself in all the arts and professions open to human skill. That indeed is one of the reasons why I have come here – out of respect for you, who are in process of showing us by your experiments what a woman is, who are in process of providing us, by your failures and successes, with that extremely important piece of information.

But to continue the story of my professional experiences. I made one pound ten and six by my first review; and I bought a Persian cat with the proceeds. Then I grew ambitious. A Persian cat is all very well, I said; but a Persian cat is not enough. I must have a motor car. And it was thus that I became a novelist – for it is a very strange thing that people will give you a motor car if you will tell them a story. It is a still stranger thing that there is nothing so delightful in the world as telling stories. It is far pleasanter than writing reviews of famous novels. And yet, if I am to obey your secretary and tell you my professional experiences as a novelist, I must tell you about a very strange experience that befell me as a novelist. And to understand it you must try first to imagine a novelist's state of mind. I hope I am not giving away professional secrets if I say that a novelist's chief desire is to be as unconscious as possible. He has to induce in himself a state of perpetual lethargy. He wants life to proceed with the utmost quiet and regularity. He wants to see the same faces, to read the same books, to do the same things day after day, month after month, while he is writing, so that nothing may break the illusion in which he is living – so that nothing may disturb or disquiet the mysterious nosings about, feelings round, darts, dashes and sudden discoveries of that very shy and illusive spirit, the imagination. I suspect that this state is the same both for men and women. Be that as it may, I want you to imagine me writing a novel in a state of trance. I want you to figure to yourselves a girl sitting with a pen in her hand, which for minutes, and indeed for hours, she never dips into the inkpot. The image that comes to my mind when I think of this girl is the image of a fisherman lying sunk in dreams on the verge of a deep lake with a rod held out over the water. She was letting her imagination sweep unchecked round every rock and cranny of the world that lies submerged in the depths of our unconscious being. Now came the experience, the experience that I believe to be far commoner with women writers than with men. The line raced through the girl's fingers. Her imagination had rushed away. It had sought the pools, the depths, the dark places where the largest fish slumber. And then there was a smash. There was an explosion. There was foam and confusion. The imagination had dashed itself against something hard. The girl was roused from her dream. She was indeed in a state of the most acute and difficult distress. To speak without figure she had thought of something, something about the body, about the passions which it was unfitting for her as a woman to say. Men, her reason told her, would be shocked. The

61

consciousness of what men will say of a woman who speaks the truth about her passions had roused her from her artist's state of unconsciousness. She could write no more. The trance was over. Her imagination could work no longer. This I believe to be a very common experience with women writers – they are impeded by the extreme conventionality of the other sex. For though men sensibly allow themselves great freedom in these respects, I doubt that they realize or can control the extreme severity with which they condemn such freedom in women.

These then were two very genuine experiences of my own. These were two of the adventures of my professional life. The first – killing the Angel in the House – I think I solved. She died. But the second, telling the truth about my own experiences as a body, I do not think I solved. I doubt that any woman has solved it yet. The obstacles against her are still immensely powerful – and yet they are very difficult to define. Outwardly, what is simpler than to write books? Outwardly, what obstacles are there for a woman rather than for a man? Inwardly, I think, the case is very different; she has still many ghosts to fight, many prejudices to overcome. Indeed it will be a long time still, I think, before a woman can sit down to write a book without finding a phantom to be slain, a rock to be dashed against. And if this is so in literature, the freest of all professions for women, how is it in the new professions which you are now for the first time entering?

Those are the questions that I should like, had I time, to ask you. And indeed, if I have laid stress upon these professional experiences of mine, it is because I believe that they are, though in different forms, yours also. Even when the path is nominally open – when there is nothing to prevent a woman from being a doctor, a lawyer, a civil servant – there are many phantoms and obstacles, as I believe, looming in her way. To discuss and define them is I think of great value and importance; for thus only can the labour be shared, the difficulties be solved. But besides this, it is necessary also to discuss the ends and the aims for which we are fighting, for which we are doing battle with these formidable obstacles. Those aims cannot be taken for granted; they must be perpetually questioned and examined. The whole position, as I see it – here in this hall surrounded by women practising for the first time in history I know not how many different professions – is one of extraordinary interest and importance. You have won rooms of your own in the house hitherto exclusively owned by men. You are able, though not without great labour and effort, to pay the rent. You are earning your five hundred pounds a year. But this freedom is only a beginning; the room is your own, but it is still bare. It has to be furnished; it has to be decorated; it has to be shared. How are you going to furnish it, how are you going to decorate it? With whom are you going to share it, and upon what terms? These, I think are questions of the utmost importance and interest. For the first time in history you are able to ask them; for the first time you are able to decide for yourselves what the answers should be. Willingly would I stay and discuss those questions and answers – but not tonight. My time is up; and I must cease.

Men and Women

This review of Léonie Villard: *La Femme Anglaise au XIXème Siècle et son Evolution d'après le Roman Anglais Contemporain* appeared in *The Times Literary Supplement*, 18 March 1920. It is reprinted in *Books and Portraits*.

If you look at a large subject through the medium of a little book you see for the most part something of such vague and wavering outline that, though it may be a Greek gem, it may almost equally be a mountain or a bathing machine. But though Mlle Villard's book is small and her subject vast, her focus is so exact and her glass so clear that the outline remains sharp and the detail distinct. Thus we can read every word with interest because it is possible at a thousand points to check her statements; she is on every page dealing with the definite and the concrete. But how, in treating of a whole century, a whole country, and a whole sex, is it possible to be either definite or concrete? Mlle Villard has solved the problem by using fiction as her material; for, though she has read Blue-books and biographies, her freshness and truth must be ascribed largely to the fact that she has preferred to read novels. In novels, she says, the thoughts, hopes and lives of women during the century and in the country of her most remarkable development are displayed more intimately and fully than elsewhere. One might indeed say that were it not for the novels of the nineteenth century we should remain as ignorant as our ancestors of this section of the human race. It has been common knowledge for ages that women exist, bear children, have no beards, and seldom go bald; but save in these respects, and in others where they are said to be identical with men, we know little of them and have little sound evidence upon which to base our conclusions. Moreover, we are seldom dispassionate.

Before the nineteenth century literature took almost solely the form of soliloquy, not of dialogue. The garrulous sex, against common repute, is not the female but the male; in all the libraries of the world the man is to be heard talking to himself and for the most part about himself. It is true that women afford ground for much speculation and are frequently represented; but it is becoming daily more evident that Lady Macbeth, Cordelia, Ophelia, Clarissa, Dora, Diana, Helen and the rest are by no means what they pretend to be. Some are plainly men in disguise; others represent what men would like to be, or are conscious of not being; or again they embody that dissatisfaction and despair which afflict most people when they reflect upon the sorry condition of the human race. To cast out and incorporate in a person of the opposite sex all that we miss in ourselves and desire in the universe and detest in humanity is a deep and universal instinct on the part both of men and of women. But though it affords relief, it does not lead to understanding. Rochester is as great a travesty of the truth about men as Cordelia is of the truth about women. Thus Mlle Villard soon finds herself confronted by the fact that some of the most famous heroines even of nineteenth-century fiction represent what men desire in women, but not necessarily what women are in themselves. Helen Pendennis, for example, tells us a great deal more about Thackeray than about herself. She tells us, indeed, that she has never had a penny that she could call her own, and no more education than serves to read the Prayer-book and the cookery-book. From her we learn also that when one sex is dependent upon the other it will endeavour for safety's sake to simulate what the dominant sex finds desirable. The women of Thackeray and the women of Dickens succeed to some extent in throwing dust in their masters' eyes, though the peculiar repulsiveness of these ladies arises from the fact that the deception is not wholly successful. The atmosphere is one of profound distrust. It is possible that Helen herself flung off her widow's weeds, took a deep draught of beer, produced a short clay pipe, and stuck her legs on the mantelpiece directly her master was round the corner. At any rate, Thackeray cannot forbear one glance of suspicion as he turns his back. But midway through the nineteenth century the servile woman was stared out of countenance by two very uncompromising characters – Jane Eyre and Isobel Berners. One insisted that she was poor and plain, and the other that she much preferred wandering on a heath to settling down and marrying anybody. Mlle Villard attributes the remarkable contrast between the servile and the defiant, the sheltered and the adventurous, to the introduction of machinery. Rather more than a century ago, after whirling for many thousands of years, the spinning-wheel became obsolete.

En fait, le désir de la femme de s'extérioriser, de dépasser les limites jusque-là assignées à son activité, prend naissance au moment même où sa vie est moins étroitement liée à toutes les heures aux tâches du foyer, aux travaux qui, une ou deux générations auparavant, absorbaient son attention et employaient ses forces. Le rouet, l'aiguille, la quenouille, la préparation des confitures et des conserves, voire des chandelles et du savon . . . n'occupent plus les femmes et, tandis que l'antique ménagère disparaît, celle qui sera demain la femme nouvelle sent grandir en elle, avec le loisir de voir, de penser, de juger, la conscience d'elle-même et du monde où elle vit.

For the first time for many ages the bent figure with the knobbed hands and the bleared eyes, who, in spite of the poets, is the true figure of womanhood, rose from her wash-tub, took a stroll out of doors, and went into the factory. That was the first painful step on the road to freedom.

Any summary of the extremely intelligent pages in which Mlle Villard has told the story of the Englishwoman's progress from 1860 to 1914 is impossible. Moreover, Mlle Villard would be the first to agree that not even a woman, and a Frenchwoman at that, looking with the clear-sighted eyes of her race across the Channel, can say for certain what the words 'emancipation' and 'evolution' amount to. Granted that the woman of the middle class has now some leisure, some education, and some liberty to investigate the world in which she lives, it will not be in this generation or in the next that she will have adjusted her position or given a clear account of her powers. 'I have the feelings of a woman,' says Bathsheba in *Far from the Madding Crowd*, 'but I have only the language of men.' From that dilemma arise infinite confusions and complications. Energy has been liberated, but into what forms is it to flow? To try the accepted forms, to discard the unfit, to create others which are more fitting, is a task that must be accomplished before there is freedom or achievement. Further, it is well to remember that woman was not created for the first time in the year 1860. A large part of her energy is already fully employed and highly developed. To pour such surplus energy as there may be into new forms without wasting a drop is the difficult problem which can only be solved by the simultaneous evolution and emancipation of man.

Women Novelists

This review of R. Brimley Johnson's *The Women
Novelists* appeared in *The Times Literary
Supplement*, 17 October 1918. It is reprinted in
Contemporary Writers.

By rights, or, more modestly, according to a
theory of ours, Mr Brimley Johnson should have written a
book amply calculated, according to the sex of the reader, to
cause gratification or annoyance, but of no value from a
critical point of view. Experience seems to prove that to
criticize the work of a sex as a sex is merely to state with
almost invariable acrimony prejudices derived from the fact
that you are either a man or a woman. By some lucky
balance of qualities Mr Brimley Johnson has delivered his
opinion of women novelists without this fatal bias, so that,
besides saying some very interesting things about literature,
he says also many that are even more interesting about the
peculiar qualities of the literature that is written by women.
Given this unusual absence of partisanship, the interest
and also the complexity of the subject can scarcely be over-
stated. Mr Johnson, who has read more novels by women
than most of us have heard of, is very cautious – more apt to
suggest than to define, and much disposed to qualify his

conclusions. Thus, though his book is not a mere study of the women novelists, but an attempt to prove that they have followed a certain course of development, we should be puzzled to state what his theory amounts to. The question is one not merely of literature, but to a large extent of social history. What, for example, was the origin of the extraordinary outburst in the eighteenth century of novel writing by women? Why did it begin then, and not in the time of the Elizabethan renaissance? Was the motive which finally determined them to write a desire to correct the current view of their sex expressed in so many volumes and for so many ages by male writers? If so, their art is at once possessed of an element which should be absent from the work of all previous writers. It is clear enough, however, that the work of Miss Burney, the mother of English fiction, was not inspired by any single wish to redress a grievance: the richness of the human scene as Dr Burney's daughter had the chance of observing it provided a sufficient stimulus; but however strong the impulse to write had become, it had at the outset to meet opposition not only of circumstance but of opinion. Her first manuscripts were burnt by her stepmother's orders, and needlework was inflicted as a penance, much as, a few years later, Jane Austen would slip her writing beneath a book if anyone came in, and Charlotte Brontë stopped in the middle of her work to pare the potatoes. But the domestic problem being overcome or compromised with, there remained the moral one. Miss Burney had showed that it was 'possible for a woman to write novels and be respectable', but the burden of proof still rested anew upon each authoress. Even so late as the mid-Victorian days George Eliot was accused of 'coarseness and immorality' in her attempt 'to familiarize the minds of our young women in the middle and higher ranks with matters on which their fathers and brothers would never venture to speak in their presence'.

The effect of these repressions is still clearly to be traced in women's work, and the effect is wholly to the bad. The

problem of art is sufficiently difficult in itself without
having to respect the ignorance of young women's minds or
to consider whether the public will think that the standard
of moral purity displayed in your work is such as they have a
right to expect from your sex. The attempt to conciliate, or
more naturally to outrage, public opinion is equally a waste
of energy and a sin against art. It may have been not
only with a view to obtaining impartial criticism that George
Eliot and Miss Brontë adopted male pseudonyms, but in
order to free their own consciousness as they wrote from the
tyranny of what was expected from their sex. No more than
men, however, could they free themselves from a more
fundamental tyranny – the tyranny of sex itself. The effort
to free themselves, or rather to enjoy what appears, perhaps
erroneously, to be the comparative freedom of the male sex
from that tyranny, is another influence which has told disastrously upon the writing of women. When Mr Brimley
Johnson says that 'imitation has not been, fortunately, the
besetting sin of women novelists', he has in mind no doubt
the work of the exceptional women who imitated neither a
sex nor any individual of either sex. But to take no more
thought of their sex when they wrote than of the colour of
their eyes was one of their conspicuous distinctions, and of
itself a proof that they wrote at the bidding of a profound
and imperious instinct. The women who wished to be taken
for men in what they wrote were certainly common enough;
and if they have given place to the women who wish to be
taken for women the change is hardly for the better, since
any emphasis, either of pride or of shame, laid consciously
upon the sex of a writer is not only irritating but superfluous. As Mr Brimley Johnson again and again remarks, a
woman's writing is always feminine; it cannot help being
feminine: the only difficulty lies in defining what we mean
by feminine. He shows his wisdom not only by advancing a
great many suggestions, but also by accepting the fact,
upsetting though it is, that women are apt to differ. Still,
here are a few attempts: 'Women are born preachers and

70

always work for an ideal.' 'Woman is the moral realist, and her realism is not inspired by any idle ideal of art, but of sympathy with life.' For all her learning, 'George Eliot's outlook remains thoroughly emotional and feminine.' Women are humorous and satirical rather than imaginative. They have a greater sense of emotional purity than men, but a less alert sense of honour.

No two people will accept without wishing to add to and qualify these attempts at a definition, and yet no one will admit that he can possibly mistake a novel written by a man for a novel written by a woman. There is the obvious and enormous difference of experience in the first place; but the essential difference lies in the fact not that men describe battles and women the birth of children, but that each sex describes itself. The first words in which either a man or a woman is described are generally enough to determine the sex of the writer; but though the absurdity of a woman's hero or of a man's heroine is universally recognized, the sexes show themselves extremely quick at detecting each other's faults. No one can deny the authenticity of a Becky Sharp or of a Mr Woodhouse. No doubt the desire and the capacity to criticize the other sex had its share in deciding women to write novels, for indeed that particular vein of comedy has been but slightly worked, and promises great richness. Then again, though men are the best judges of men and women of women, there is a side of each sex which is known only to the other, nor does this refer solely to the relationship of love. And finally (as regards this review at least) there rises for consideration the very difficult question of the difference between the man's and the woman's view of what constitutes the importance of any subject. From this spring not only marked differences of plot and incident, but infinite differences in selection, method and style.

71

Indiscretions

This article in *Vogue*, November 1924, reveals a lighter side of Virginia Woolf's journalism. It was subtitled ' "Never Seek to Tell Thy Love, Love That Never Told Can Be" – but One's Feelings for Some Writers Outrun all Prudence'.

It is always indiscreet to mention the affections. Yet how they prevail, how they permeate all our intercourse! Boarding an omnibus we like the conductor; in a shop take for or against the young lady serving; through all traffic and routine, liking and disliking we go our ways, and our whole day is stained and steeped by the affections. And so it must be in reading. The critic may be able to abstract the essence and feast upon it undisturbed, but for the rest of us in every book there is something – sex, character, temperament – which, as in life, rouses affection or repulsion; and, as in life, sways and prejudices; and again, as in life, is hardly to be analysed by the reason.

George Eliot is a case in point. Her reputation, they say, is on the wane, and, indeed, how could it be otherwise? Her big nose, her little eyes, her heavy, horsey head loom from behind the printed page and make a critic of the other sex uneasy. Praise he must, but love he cannot; and however absolute and austere his devotion to the principle that art has no truck with personality, still there has crept into his voice, into textbooks and articles, as he analyses her gifts and unmasks her pretentions, that it is not George Eliot he would like to pour out tea. On the other hand, exquisitely and urbanely, from the chastest urn into the finest china Jane Austen pours, and, as she pours, smiles, charms, appreciates – that too has made its way into the austere pages of English criticism.

But now perhaps it may be pertinent, since women not only read but sometimes scribble a note of their opinions, to enquire into their preferences, their equally suppressed but equally instinctive response to the lure of personal liking in the printed page. The attractions and repulsions of sex are naturally among the most emphatic. One may hear them crackling and spitting and lending an agreeable vivacity to the insipidity of weekly journalism. In higher spheres these same impurities serve to fledge the arrows and wing the mind more swiftly if more capriciously in its flight. Some adjustment before reading is essential. Byron is the first name that comes to mind. But no woman ever loved Byron; they bowed to convention; did what they were told to do; ran mad to order. Intolerably condescending, ineffably vain, a barber's block to look at, compound of bully and lap-dog, now hectoring, now swimming in vapours of sentimental twaddle, tedious, egotistical, melodramatic, the character of Byron is the least attractive in the history of letters. But no wonder that every man was in love with him. In their company he must have been irresistible; brilliant and courageous; dashing and satirical; downright and tremendous; the conquerer of women and companion of heroes – everything that strong men believe themselves to be and weak men envy them for being. But to fall in love with Byron, to enjoy Don Juan and the letters to the full, obviously one must be a man; or, if of the other sex, disguise it.

No such disguise is necessary with Keats. His name, indeed, is to be mentioned with diffidence lest the thought of a character endowed as his was with the rarest qualities that human beings can command – genius, sensibility, dignity, wisdom – should mislead us into mere panegyric. There, if ever, was a man whom both sexes must unite to honour; towards whom the personal bias must incline all in the same direction. But there is a hitch; there is Fanny Brawne. She danced too much at Hampstead, Keats complained. The divine poet was a little sultanic in his behaviour; after the manly fashion of his time apt to treat his adored both as angel and cockatoo. A jury of maidens would bring in a verdict in Fanny's favour. It was to his sister, whose education he supervised and whose character he formed, that he showed himself the man of all others who 'had he been put on would have prov'd most royally'. Sisterly his women readers must suppose themselves to be; and sisterly to Wordsworth, who should have had no wife, as Tennyson should have had none, nor Charlotte Brontë her Mr Nicholls.

To put oneself at the best post of observation for the study of Samuel Johnson needs a little circumspection. He was apt to tear the tablecloth to ribbons; he was a disciplinarian and a sentimentalist; very rude to women, and at the same time the most devoted, respectful and devout of their admirers. Neither Mrs Thrale, whom he harangued, nor the pretty young woman who sat on his knee is to be envied altogether. Their positions are too precarious. But some sturdy match-seller or apple woman well on in years, some old struggler who had won for herself a decent independence would have commanded his sympathy, and, standing at a stall on a rainy night in the Strand, one might perhaps have insinuated oneself into his service, washed up his tea cups and thus enjoyed the greatest felicity that could fall to the lot of woman.

These instances, however, are all of a simple character; the men have been supposed to remain men, the women women when they write. They have exerted the influence of their sex directly and normally. But there is a class which keeps itself aloof from any such contamination. Milton is their leader; with him are Landor, Sappho, Sir Thomas

Browne, Marvell. Feminists or anti-feminists, passionate or cold – whatever the romances or adventures of their private lives not a whiff of that mist attaches itself to their writing. It is pure, uncontaminated, sexless as the angels are said to be sexless. But on no account is this to be confused with another group which has the same peculiarity. To which sex do the works of Emerson, Matthew Arnold, Harriet Martineau, Ruskin and Maria Edgeworth belong? It is uncertain. It is, moreover, quite immaterial. They are not men when they write, nor are they women. They appeal to the large tract of the soul which is sexless; they excite no passions; they exalt, improve, instruct, and man or woman can profit equally by their pages, without indulging in the folly of affection or the fury of partisanship.

Then, inevitably, we come to the harem, and tremble slightly as we approach the curtain and catch glimpses of women behind it and even hear ripples of laughter and snatches of conversation. Some obscurity still veils the relations of women to each other. A hundred years ago it was simple enough; they were stars who shone only in male sunshine; deprived of it, they languished into nonentity – sniffed, bickered, envied each other – so men said. But now it must be confessed things are less satisfactory. Passions and repulsions manifest themselves here too, and it is by no means certain that every woman is inspired by pure envy when she reads what another has written. More probably Emily Brontë was the passion of her youth; Charlotte even she loved with nervous affection; and cherished a quiet sisterly regard for Anne. Mrs Gaskell wields a maternal sway over readers of her own sex; wise, witty and very large-minded, her readers are devoted to her as to the most admirable of mothers; whereas George Eliot is an Aunt, and, as an Aunt, inimitable. So treated she drops the apparatus of masculinity which Herbert Spencer necessitated; indulges herself in memory; and pours forth, no doubt with some rustic accent, the genial stores of her youth, the greatness and profundity of her soul. Jane

Austen we needs must adore; but she does not want it; she wants nothing; our love is a by-product, an irrelevance; with that mist or without it her moon shines on. As for loving foreigners, some say it is an impossibility; but if not, it is to Madame de Sévigné that we must turn.

But all these preferences and partialities, all these adjustments and attempts of the mind to relate itself harmoniously with another, pale, as the flirtations of a summer compared with the consuming passions of a lifetime, when we consider the great devotions which one, or at most two, names in the whole of literature inspire. Of Shakespeare we need not speak. The nimble little birds of field and hedge, lizards, shrews and dormice, do not pause in their dallying and sportings to thank the sun for warming them; nor need we, the light of whose literature comes from Shakespeare, seek to praise him. But there are other names, more retired, less central, less universally gazed upon than his. There is a poet, whose love of women was all stuck about with briars; who railed and cursed; was fierce and tender; passionate and obscene. In the very obscurity of his mind there is something that intrigues us on; his rage scorches but sets on fire; and in the thickest of his thorn bushes are glimpses of the highest heavens, and ecstasies and pure and windless calms. Whether as a young man gazing from narrow Chinese eyes upon a world that half allures, half disgusts him, or with his flesh dried on his cheek bones, wrapped in his winding sheet, excruciated, dead in St Paul's, one cannot help but love John Donne. With him is associated a man of the very opposite sort – large, lame, simple-minded; a scribbler of innumerable novels not a line of which is harsh, obscure or anything but propriety itself; a landed gentleman with a passion for Gothic architecture; a man who, if he had lived today, would have been the upholder of all the most detestable institutions of his country, but for all that a great writer – no woman can read the life of this man and his diary and his novels without being head over ears in love with Walter Scott.

PART TWO

PART TWO

The Duchess of Newcastle

Margaret Cavendish, Duchess of Newcastle (1624?–74)
This essay was published in *The Common Reader:* First Series with a note by Virginia Woolf referring to *The Life of William Cavendish, Duke of Newcastle, Etc.,* edited by C. H. Firth; *Poems and Fancies,* by the Duchess of Newcastle; *The World's Oho, Orations of divers Sorts Accommodated to Divers Places*; *Female Orations*; *Plays*; *Philosophical Letters, etc., etc.* Virginia Woolf had reviewed Thomas Longueville's *The First Duke and Duchess of Newcastle-Upon-Tyne* in *The Times Literary Supplement,* 2 February 1911.

'. . . All I desire is fame', wrote Margaret Cavendish, Duchess of Newcastle. And while she lived her wish was granted. Garish in her dress, eccentric in her habits, chaste in her conduct, coarse in her speech, she succeeded during her lifetime in drawing upon herself the ridicule of the great and the applause of the learned. But the last echoes of that clamour have now all died away; she lives only in the few splendid phrases that Lamb scattered upon her tomb; her poems, her plays, her philosophies, her orations, her discourses – all these folios and quartos in which, she protested, her real life was shrined – moulder in the gloom of public libraries, or are decanted into tiny thimbles which hold six drops of their profusion. Even the curious student, inspired by the words of Lamb, quails before the mass of her mausoleum, peers in, looks about him, and hurries out again, shutting the door.

But the hasty glance has shown him the outlines of a memorable figure. Born (it is conjectured) in 1624,

Margaret was the youngest child of Thomas Lucas, who died when she was an infant, and her upbringing was due to her mother, a lady of remarkable character, of majestic grandeur and beauty 'beyond the ruin of time'. 'She was very skilful in leases, and setting of lands and court keeping, ordering of stewards, and the like affairs.' The wealth which thus accrued she spent, not on marriage portions, but on generous and delightful pleasures, 'out of an opinion that if she bred us with needy necessity it might chance to create in us sharking qualities'. Her eight sons and daughters were never beaten, but reasoned with, finely and gaily dressed, and allowed no conversation with servants, not because they are servants but because servants 'are for the most part ill-bred as well as meanly born'. The daughters were taught the usual accomplishments 'rather for formality than for benefit', it being their mother's opinion that character, happiness, and honesty were of greater value to a woman than fiddling and singing, or 'the prating of several languages'.

Already Margaret was eager to take advantage of such indulgence to gratify certain tastes. Already she liked reading better than needlework, dressing and 'inventing fashions' better than reading, and writing best of all. Sixteen paper books of no title, written in straggling letters, for the impetuosity of her thought always outdid the pace of her fingers, testify to the use she made of her mother's liberality. The happiness of their home life had other results as well. They were a devoted family. Long after they were married, Margaret noted, these handsome brothers and sisters, with their well-proportioned bodies, their clear complexions, brown hair, sound teeth, 'tunable voices', and plain way of speaking, kept themselves 'in a flock together'. The presence of strangers silenced them. But when they were alone, whether they walked in Spring Gardens or Hyde Park, or had music, or supped in barges upon the water, their tongues were loosed and they made 'very merry amongst themselves, . . . judging, condemning, approving, commending, as they thought good'.

The happy family life had its effect upon Margaret's character. As a child, she would walk for hours alone, musing and contemplating and reasoning with herself of 'everything her senses did present'. She took no pleasure in activity of any kind. Toys did not amuse her, and she could neither learn foreign languages nor dress as other people did. Her great pleasure was to invent dresses for herself, which nobody else was to copy, 'for', she remarks, 'I always took delight in a singularity, even in accoutrements of habits'.

Such a training, at once so cloistered and so free, should have bred a lettered old maid, glad of her seclusion, and the writer perhaps of some volume of letters or translations from the classics, which we should still quote as proof of the cultivation of our ancestresses. But there was a wild streak in Margaret, a love of finery and extravagance and fame, which was for ever upsetting the orderly arrangements of nature. When she heard that the Queen, since the outbreak of the Civil War, had fewer maids-of-honour than usual, she had 'a great desire' to become one of them. Her mother let her go against the judgement of the rest of the family, who, knowing that she had never left home and had scarcely been beyond their sight, justly thought that she might behave at Court to her disadvantage. 'Which indeed I did,' Margaret confessed; 'for I was so bashful when I was out of my mother's, brothers', and sisters' sight that . . . I durst neither look up with my eyes, nor speak, nor be any way sociable, insomuch as I was thought a natural fool.' The courtiers laughed at her; and she retaliated in the obvious way. People were censorious; men were jealous of brains in a woman; women suspected intellect in their own sex; and what other lady, she might justly ask, pondered as she walked on the nature of matter and whether snails have teeth? But the laughter galled her, and she begged her mother to let her come home. This being refused, wisely as the event turned out, she stayed on for two years (1643–45), finally going with the Queen to Paris, and there, among the

81

exiles who came to pay their respects to the Court, was the Marquis of Newcastle. To the general amazement, the princely nobleman, who had led the King's forces to disaster with indomitable courage but little skill, fell in love with the shy, silent, strangely dressed maid-of-honour. It was not 'amorous love, but honest, honourable love', according to Margaret. She was no brilliant match; she had gained a reputation for prudery and eccentricity. What, then, could have made so great a nobleman fall at her feet? The onlookers were full of derision, disparagement, and slander. 'I fear,' Margaret wrote to the Marquis, 'others foresee we shall be unfortunate, though we see it not ourselves, or else there would not be such pains to untie the knot of our affections.' Again, 'Saint Germains is a place of much slander, and thinks I send too often to you'. 'Pray consider', she warned him, 'that I have enemies.' But the match was evidently perfect. The Duke, with his love of poetry and music and play-writing, his interest in philosophy, his belief 'that nobody knew or could know the cause of anything', his romantic and generous temperament, was naturally drawn to a woman who wrote poetry herself, was also a philosopher of the same way of thinking, and lavished upon him not only the admiration of a fellow-artist, but the gratitude of a sensitive creature who had been shielded and succoured by his extraordinary magnanimity. 'He did approve', she wrote, 'of those bashful fears which many condemned, . . . and though I did dread marriage and shunned men's company as much as I could, yet I . . . had not the power to refuse him.' She kept him company during the long years of exile; she entered with sympathy, if not with understanding, into the conduct and acquirements of those horses which he trained to such perfection that the Spaniards crossed themselves and cried 'Miraculo!' as they witnessed their corvets, voltoes, and pirouettes; she believed that the horses even made a 'trampling action' for joy when he came into the stables; she pleaded his cause in England during the Protectorate; and, when the Restoration made it possible for them to return to England, they lived together in the depths of the country in the greatest seclusion and perfect contentment, scribbling plays, poems, philosophies, greeting each other's works with raptures of delight, and confabulating, doubtless, upon such marvels of the natural world as chance threw their way. They were laughed at by their contemporaries; Horace Walpole sneered at them. But there can be no doubt that they were perfectly happy.

For now Margaret could apply herself uninterruptedly to her writing. She could devise fashions for herself and her servants. She could scribble more and more furiously with fingers that became less and less able to form legible letters. She could even achieve the miracle of getting her plays acted in London and her philosophies humbly perused by men of learning. There they stand, in the British Museum, volume after volume, swarming with a diffused, uneasy, contorted vitality. Order, continuity, the logical development of her argument are all unknown to her. No fears impede her. She has the irresponsibility of a child and the arrogance of a Duchess. The wildest fancies come to her, and she canters away on their backs. We seem to hear her, as the thoughts boil and bubble, calling to John, who sat with a pen in his hand next door, to come quick, 'John, John, I conceive!' And down it goes – whatever it may be; sense or nonsense; some thought on women's education – 'Women live like Bats or Owls, labour like Beasts, and die like Worms, . . . the best bred women are those whose minds are civilest'; some speculation that had struck her, perhaps, walking that afternoon alone – why 'hogs have the measles', why 'dogs that rejoice swing their tails', or what the stars are made of, or what this chrysalis is that her maid has brought her, and she keeps warm in a corner of her room. On and on, from subject to subject she flies, never stopping to correct, 'for there is more pleasure in making than in mending', talking aloud to herself of all those matters that filled her brain to her perpetual diversion – of wars, and boarding-schools, and cutting down trees, of grammar and morals, of monsters and the British, whether opium in small quantities is good for lunatics, why it is that musicians are mad. Looking upwards, she speculates still more ambitiously upon the nature of the moon, and if the stars are blazing jellies; looking downwards she wonders if the fishes know that the sea is salt; opines that our heads are full of fairies, 'dear to God as we are'; muses whether there are not other worlds than ours, and reflects that the next ship may bring us word of a new one. In short, 'we are in utter darkness'. Meanwhile, what a rapture is thought!

As the vast books appeared from the stately retreat at Welbeck the usual censors made the usual objections, and had to be answered, despised, or argued with, as her mood varied, in the preface to every work. They said, among other things, that her books were not her own, because she used learned terms, and 'wrote of many matters outside her ken'. She flew to her husband for help, and he answered, characteristically, that the Duchess 'had never conversed with any professed scholar in learning except her brother and myself'. The Duke's scholarship, moreover, was of a peculiar nature. 'I have lived in the great world a great while, and have thought of what has been brought to me by the senses, more than was put into me by learned discourse; for I do not love to be led by the nose, by authority, and old authors; *ipse dixit* will not serve my turn.' And then she takes up the pen and proceeds, with the importunity and indiscretion of a child, to assure the world that her ignorance is of the finest quality imaginable. She has only seen Des Cartes and Hobbes, not questioned them; she did indeed ask Mr Hobbes to dinner, but he could not come; she often does not listen to a word that is said to her; she does not know any French, though she lived abroad for five years; she has only read the old philosophers in Mr Stanley's account of them; of Des Cartes she has read but half of his work on Passion; and of Hobbes only 'the little book called *De Cive*', all of which is infinitely to the credit of her native wit, so abundant that outside succour pained it, so honest that it would not accept help from others. It was from the plain of complete ignorance, the untilled field of her own consciousness, that she proposed to erect a philosophic system that was to oust all others. The results were not altogether happy. Under the pressure of such vast structures, her natural gift, the fresh and delicate fancy which had led her in her first volume to write charmingly of Queen Mab and fairyland, was crushed out of existence.

> The palace of the Queen wherein she dwells,
> Its fabric's built all of hodmandod shells;
> The hangings of a Rainbow made that's thin,
> Shew wondrous fine, when one first enters in;
> The chambers made of Amber that is clear,
> Do give a fine sweet smell, if fire be near;
> Her bed a cherry stone, is carved throughout,
> And with a butterfly's wing hung about;
> Her sheets are of the skin of Dove's eyes made
> Where on a violet bud her pillow's laid.

So she could write when she was young. But her fairies, if they survived at all, grew up into hippopotami. Too generously her prayer was granted:

> Give me the free and noble style,
> Which seems uncurb'd, though it be wild.

She became capable of involutions, and contortions and conceits of which the following is among the shortest, but not the most terrific:

> The human head may be likened to a town:
> The mouth when full, begun
> Is market day, when empty, market's done;
> The city conduct, where the water flows,
> Is with two spouts, the nostrils and the nose.

She similised, energetically, incongruously, eternally; the sea became a meadow, the sailors shepherds, the mast a maypole. The fly was the bird of summer, trees were senators, houses ships, and even the fairies, whom she loved better than any earthly thing, except the Duke, are changed into blunt atoms and sharp atoms, and take part in some of those horrible manoeuvres in which she delighted to marshal the universe. Truly, 'my Lady Sanspareille hath a strange spreading wit'. Worse still, without an atom of dramatic power, she turned to play-writing. It was a simple process. The unwieldly thoughts which turned and tumbled within her were christened Sir Golden Riches, Moll Meanbred, Sir Puppy Dogman, and the rest, and sent revolving in tedious debate upon the parts of the soul, or whether virtue is better than riches, round a wise and learned lady who answered their questions and corrected their fallacies at considerable length in tones which we seem to have heard before.

Sometimes, however, the Duchess walked abroad. She would issue out in her own proper person, dressed in a thousand gems and furbelows, to visit the houses of the neighbouring gentry. Her pen made instant report of these excursions. She recorded how Lady C.R. 'did beat her husband in a public assembly'; Sir F.O. 'I am sorry to hear hath undervalued himself so much below his birth and wealth as to marry his kitchen-maid'; 'Miss P.I. has become a sanctified soul, a spiritual sister, she has left curling her hair, black patches are become abominable to her, laced shoes and Galoshoes are steps to pride – she asked me what posture I thought was the best to be used in prayer.' Her answer was probably unacceptable. 'I shall not rashly go there again,' she says of one such 'gossip-making'. She was not, we may hazard, a welcome guest or an altogether hospitable hostess. She had a way of 'bragging of myself' which frightened visitors so that they left, nor was she sorry to see them go. Indeed, Welbeck was the best place for her, and her own company the most congenial, with the amiable

Duke wandering in and out, with his plays and his speculations, always ready to answer a question or refute a slander. Perhaps it was this solitude that led her, chaste as she was in conduct, to use language which in time to come much perturbed Sir Egerton Brydges. She used, he complained, 'expressions and images of extraordinary coarseness as flowing from a female of high rank brought up in courts'. He forgot that this particular female had long ceased to frequent the Court; she consorted chiefly with fairies; and her friends were among the dead. Naturally, then, her language was coarse. Nevertheless, though her philosophies are futile, and her plays intolerable, and her verses mainly dull, the vast bulk of the Duchess is leavened by a vein of authentic fire. One cannot help following the lure of her erratic and lovable personality as it meanders and twinkles through page after page. There is something noble and Quixotic and high-spirited, as well as crack-brained and bird-witted, about her. Her simplicity is so open; her intelligence so active; her sympathy with fairies and animals so true and tender. She has the freakishness of an elf, the irresponsibility of some non-human creature, its heartlessness, and its charm. And although 'they', those terrible critics who had sneered and jeered at her ever since, as a shy girl, she had not dared look her tormentors in the face at Court, continued to mock, few of her critics, after all, had the wit to trouble about the nature of the universe, or cared a straw for the sufferings of the hunted hare, or longed, as she did, to talk to some one 'of Shakespeare's fools'. Now, at any rate, the laugh is not all on their side.

But laugh they did. When the rumour spread that the crazy Duchess was coming up from Welbeck to pay her respects at Court, people crowded the streets to look at her, and the curiosity of Mr Pepys twice brought him to wait in the Park to see her pass. But the pressure of the crowd about her coach was too great. He could only catch a glimpse of her in her silver coach with her footmen all in velvet, a velvet cap on her head, and her hair about her ears. He could only see for a moment between the white curtains the face of 'a very comely woman', and on she drove through the crowd of staring Cockneys, all pressing to catch a glimpse of that romantic lady, who stands, in the picture of Welbeck, with large melancholy eyes, and something fastidious and fantastic in her bearing, touching a table with the tips of long pointed fingers, in the calm assurance of immortal fame.

Aphra Behn

Aphra Behn (1640–89) was reportedly the first woman to earn a living by writing (having been widowed at the age of twenty-six). As such she marks an important point in the argument of *A Room of One's Own*, from which this passage is extracted.

. . . With Mrs Behn we turn a very important corner on the road. We leave behind, shut up in their parks among their folios, those solitary great ladies who wrote without audience or criticism, for their own delight alone. We come to town and rub shoulders with ordinary people in the streets. Mrs Behn was a middle-class woman with all the plebeian virtues of humour, vitality, and courage; a woman forced by the death of her husband and some unfortunate adventures of her own to make her living by her wits. She had to work on equal terms with men. She made, by working very hard, enough to live on. The importance of that fact outweighs anything that she actually wrote, even the splendid *A Thousand Martyrs I have made*, or *Love in Fantastic Triumph sat*, for here begins the freedom of the mind, or rather the possiblity that in the course of time the mind will be free to write what it likes. For now that Aphra Behn had done it, girls could go to their parents and say, You need not give me an allowance; I can make money by my pen. Of course the answer for many years to come was, Yes, by living the life of Aphra Behn! Death would be better! and the door was slammed faster than ever. That profoundly interesting subject, the value that men set upon women's chastity and its effect upon their education, here suggests itself for discussion, and might provide an interesting book if any student at Girton or Newnham cared to go into the matter. Lady Dudley, sitting in diamonds among the midges of a Scottish moor, might serve for frontispiece. Lord Dudley, *The Times* said when Lady Dudley died the other day, 'a man of cultivated taste and many accomplishments, was benevolent and bountiful, but whimsically despotic. He insisted upon his wife's wearing full dress, even at the remotest shooting-lodge in the Highlands; he loaded her with gorgeous jewels', and so on, 'he gave her everything – always excepting any measure of responsibility'. Then Lord Dudley had a stroke and she nursed him and ruled his estates with supreme competence for ever after. That whimsical despotism was in the nineteenth century too.

But to return. Aphra Behn proved that money could be made by writing at the sacrifice, perhaps, of certain agreeable qualities; and so by degrees writing became not merely a sign of folly and a distracted mind, but was of practical importance. A husband might die, or some disaster overtake the family. Hundreds of women began as the eighteenth century drew on to add to their pin money, or to come to the rescue of their families by making translations or writing the innumerable bad novels which have ceased to be recorded even in text-books, but are to be picked up in the fourpenny boxes in the Charing Cross Road. The extreme activity of mind which showed itself in the later eighteenth century among women – the talking, and the meeting, the writing of essays on Shakespeare, the translating of the classics – was founded on the solid fact that women could make money by writing. Money dignifies what is frivolous if unpaid for. It might still be well to sneer at 'blue stockings with an itch for scribbling', but it could not be denied that they could put money in their purses. Thus, towards the end of the eighteenth century a change came about which, if I were rewriting history, I should describe more fully and think of greater importance than the Crusades or the Wars of the Roses. The middle-class woman began to write. For if *Pride and Prejudice* matters, and *Middlemarch* and *Villette* and *Wuthering Heights* matter, then it matters far more than I can prove in a hour's discourse that women generally, and not merely the lonely aristocrat shut up in her country house among her folios and her flatterers, took to writing. Without those forerunners, Jane Austen and the Brontës and George Eliot could no more have written than Shakespeare could have written without Marlowe, or Marlowe without Chaucer, or Chaucer without those forgotten poets who paved the ways and tamed the natural savagery of the tongue. For masterpieces are not single and solitary births; they are the outcome of many years of thinking in common, of thinking by the body of the people, so that the experience of the mass is behind the single voice. Jane Austen should have laid a wreath upon the grave of Fanny Burney, and George Eliot done homage to the robust shade of Eliza Carter – the valiant old woman who tied a bell to her bedstead in order that she might wake early and learn Greek. All women together ought to let flowers fall upon the tomb of Aphra Behn, which is, most scandalously but rather appropriately, in Westminster Abbey, for it was she who earned them the right to speak their minds. It is she – shady and amorous as she was – who makes it not quite fantastic for me to say to you tonight: Earn five hundred a year by your wits.

A Scribbling Dame

(ELIZA HAYWOOD)

Eliza Haywood (1693–1756)
This review of *The Life and Romances of Mrs
Eliza Haywood*, by George F. Whicher,
appeared in *The Times Literary Supplement* of 17
February 1916. It is reprinted in *Books and
Portraits*.

There are in the Naural History Museum certain
little insects so small that they have to be gummed to the
cardboard with the lightest of fingers, but each of them, as
one observes with constant surprise, has its fine Latin name
spreading far to the right and left of the miniature body. We
have often speculated upon the capture of these insects and
the christening of them, and marvelled at the labours of the
humble, indefatigable men who thus extend our knowledge.
But their toil, though comparable in its nature, seems light
and certainly agreeable compared with that of Mr Whicher
in the book before us. It was not for him to wander through
airy forests with a butterfly net in his hand; he had to search
out dusty books from desolate museums, and in the end to
pin down this faded and antique specimen of the domestic
house fly with all her seventy volumes in orderly array
around her. But it appears to the Department of English and
Comparative Literature in Columbia University that Mrs
Haywood has never been classified, and they approve there-

fore of the publication of this book on her as 'a contribution to knowledge worthy of publication'. It does not matter, presumably, that she was a writer of no importance, that no one read her for pleasure, and that nothing is known of her life. She is dead, she is old, she wrote books, and nobody has yet written a book about her.

Mr Whicher accordingly has supplied not merely an article, or a few lines in a history of literature, but a careful, studious, detailed account of all her works regarded from every possible point of view, together with a bibliography which occupies 204 pages of print. It is but fair to him to add that he has few illusions as to the merits of his authoress, and only claims for her that her 'domestic novels' foreshadowed the work of Miss Burney and Miss Austen, and that she helped to open a new profession for her sex. Whatever help he can afford us by calling Pope 'Mr' Pope or Pope Alexander, and alluding to Mrs Haywood as 'the scribbling dame', he proffers generously enough. But it is scarcely sufficient. If he had been able to throw any light upon the circumstances of her life we should make no complaint. A woman who married a clergyman and ran away from him, who supported herself and possibly two children, it is thought without gallantry, entirely by her pen in the early years of the eighteenth century, was striking out a new line of life and must have been a person of character. But nobody knows anything about her, save that she was born in 1693 and died in 1756; it is not known where she lived or how she got her work; what friends she had, or even, which is strange in the case of a woman, whether she was plain or handsome. 'The apprehensive dame,' as Mr Whicher calls her, warned, we can imagine, by the disgusting stanzas in the 'Dunciad', took care that the facts of her life should be concealed, and, withdrawing silently, left behind her a mass of unreadable journalism which both by its form and by the inferiority of the writer's talent throws no light upon her age or upon herself. Anyone who has looked into the works of the Duchess of Newcastle and Mrs Behn knows how easily the rich prose style of the Restoration tends to fall languid and suffocate even writers of considerable force and originality. The names alone of Mrs Haywood's romances make us droop, and in the mazes of her plots we swoon away. We have to imagine how Emilia wandering in Andalusia meets Berinthus in a masquerade. Now Berinthus was really Henriquez her brother. . . . Don Jaque di Morella determines to marry his daughter Clementine to a certain cardinal. . . . . In Montelupe Clementina meets the funeral of a young woman who has been torn to pieces by wolves. . . . The young and gay Dorante is tempted to expose himself to the charms of the beautiful Kesiah. . . . The doting Baron de Tortillés marries the extravagant and lascivious Mademoiselle la Motte. . . . Melliora, Placentia, Montrano, Miramillia, and a thousand more swarm over all the countries of the South and of the East, climbing ropes, dropping letters, overhearing secrets, plunging daggers, languishing and dying, fighting and conquering, but loving, always loving, for, as Mr Whicher puts it, to Mrs Haywood 'love was the force that motivated all the world'.

These stories found certain idle people very ready to read them, and were generally successful. Mrs Haywood was evidently a born journalist. As long as romances of the heart were in fashion she turned out romance after romance; when Richardson and Fielding brought the novel into closer touch with life she followed suit with her *Miss Betsy Thoughtless* and her *Jemmy and Jenny Jessamy*. In the interval she turned publisher, edited a newspaper called *The Parrot*, and produced secret histories and scandal novels rather in the style of our gossip in the illustrated papers about the aristocracy. In none of these departments was she a pioneer, or even a very distinguished disciple; and it is more for her steady industry with the pen than for the product of it that she is remarkable. Reading when Mrs Haywood wrote was beginning to come into fashion, and readers demanded books which they could read 'with a tea-cup in one hand without danger of spilling the tea'. But that class, as Mr Gosse indicates when he compares Mrs Haywood to Ouida, has not been improved away nor lessened in numbers. There is the same desire to escape from the familiar look of life by the easiest way, and the difference is really that we find our romance in accumulated motor-cars and marquises rather than in foreign parts and strange-sounding names. But the heart which suffered in the pages of the early romancers beats today upon the railway book-stall beneath the shiny coloured cover which depicts Lord Belcour parting from the Lady Belinda Fitzurse, or the Duchess of Ormonde clasping the family diamonds and bathed in her own blood at the bottom of the marble staircase.

In what sense Mr Whicher can claim that Mrs Haywood 'prepared the way for . . . quiet Jane Austen' it is difficult to see, save that one lady was undeniably born some eighty years in advance of the other. For it would be hard to imagine a less professional woman of letters than the lady who wrote on little slips of paper, hid them when anyone was near, and kept her novels shut up in her desk, and refused to write a romance about the august House of Coburg at the suggestion of Prince Leopold's lib-rarian – behaviour that must have made Mrs Haywood lift her hands in amazement in the grave. And in that long and very intricate process of living and reading and writing which so mysteriously alters the form of literature, so that Jane Austen, born in 1775, wrote novels, while Jane Austen born a hundred years earlier would probably have written not novels but a few exquisite lost letters, Mrs Haywood plays no perceptible part, save that of swelling the chorus of sound. For people who write books do not necessarily add anything to the history of literature, even when those books are little old volumes, stained with age, that have crossed the Atlantic; nor can we see that the students of Columbia University will love English literature the better for know-ing how very dull it can be, although the University may claim that this is a 'contribution to knowledge'.

Mary Wollstonecraft

Mary Wollstonecraft (1759–97), author of
Vindication of the Rights of Woman, 1792
This essay was published in *The Common
Reader:* Second Series as one of 'Four Figures'. It
was originally written for the *Nation and
Athenaeum*, 5 October 1929.

Great wars are strangely intermittent in their
effects. The French Revolution took some people and tore
them asunder; others it passed over without disturbing a
hair of their heads. Jane Austen, it is said, never mentioned
it; Charles Lamb ignored it; Beau Brummell never gave the
matter a thought. But to Wordsworth and to Godwin it was
the dawn; unmistakably they saw

France standing on the top of golden hours,
And human nature seeming born again.

Thus it would be easy for a picturesque historian to lay side
by side the most glaring contrasts – here in Chesterfield
Street was Beau Brummell letting his chin fall carefully upon
his cravat and discussing in a tone studiously free from
vulgar emphasis the proper cut of the lapel of a coat; and
here in Somers Town was a party of ill-dressed, excited
young men, one with a head too big for his body and a nose

too long for his face, holding forth day by day over the tea-cups upon human perfectibility, ideal unity, and the rights of man. There was also a woman present with very bright eyes and a very eager tongue, and the young men, who had middle-class names, like Barlow and Holcroft and Godwin, called her simply 'Wollstonecraft', as if it did not matter whether she were married or unmarried, as if she were a young man like themselves.

Such glaring discords among intelligent people – for Charles Lamb and Godwin, Jane Austen and Mary Wollstonecraft were all highly intelligent – suggest how much influence circumstances have upon opinions. If Godwin had been brought up in the precincts of the Temple and had drunk deep of antiquity and old letters at Christ's Hospital, he might never have cared a straw for the future of man and his rights in general. If Jane Austen had lain as a child on the landing to prevent her father from thrashing her mother, her soul might have burnt with such a passion against tyranny that all her novels might have been consumed in one cry for justice.

Such had been Mary Wollstonecraft's first experience of the joys of married life. And then her sister Everina had been married miserably and had bitten her wedding ring to pieces in the coach. Her brother had been a burden on her; her father's farm had failed, and in order to start that disreputable man with the red face and the violent temper and the dirty hair in life again she had gone into bondage among the aristocracy as a governess – in short, she had never known what happiness was, and, in its default, had fabricated a creed fitted to meet the sordid misery of real human life. The staple of her doctrine was that nothing mattered save independence. 'Every obligation we receive from our fellow-creatures is a new shackle, takes from our native freedom, and debases the mind.' Independence was the first necessity for a woman; not grace or charm, but energy and courage and the power to put her will into effect, were her necessary qualities. It was her highest boast to be able to say, 'I never yet resolved to do anything of consequence that I did not adhere readily to it.' Certainly Mary could say this with truth. When she was a little more than thirty she could look back upon a series of actions which she had carried out in the teeth of opposition. She had taken a house by prodigious efforts for her friend Fanny, only to find that Fanny's mind was changed and she did not want a house after all. She had started a school. She had persuaded Fanny into marrying Mr Skeys. She had thrown up her school and gone to Lisbon alone to nurse Fanny when she died. On the voyage back she had forced the captain of the ship to rescue a wrecked French vessel by threatening to expose him if he refused. And when, overcome by a passion for Fuseli, she declared her wish to live with him and been refused flatly by his wife, she had put her principle of decisive action instantly into effect, and had gone to Paris determined to make her living by her pen.

The Revolution thus was not merely an event that had happened outside her; it was an active agent in her own blood. She had been in revolt all her life – against tyranny, against law, against convention. The reformer's love of humanity, which has so much of hatred in it as well as love, fermented within her. The outbreak of revolution in France expressed some of her deepest theories and convictions, and she dashed off in the heat of that extraordinary moment those two eloquent and daring books – the *Reply to Burke* and the *Vindication of the Rights of Woman,* which are so true that they seem now to contain nothing new in them – their originality has become our commonplace. But when she was in Paris lodging by herself in a great house, and saw with her own eyes the King whom she depised driving past surrounded by National Guards and holding himself with greater dignity than she expected, then, 'I can scarcely tell you why', the tears came to her eyes. 'I am going to bed,' the letter ended, 'and, for the first time in my life, I cannot put out the candle.' Things were not so simple after all. She could not understand even her own feelings.

She saw the most cherished of her convictions put into practice – and her eyes filled with tears. She had won fame and independence and the right to live her own life – and she wanted something different. 'I do not want to be loved like a goddess,' she wrote, 'but I wish to be necessary to you.' For Imlay, the fascinating American to whom her letter was addressed, had been very good to her. Indeed, she had fallen passionately in love with him. But it was one of her theories that love should be free – 'that mutual affection was marriage and that the marriage tie should not bind after the death of love, if love should die'. And yet at the same time that she wanted freedom she wanted certainty. 'I like the word affection,' she wrote, 'because it signifies something habitual.'

The conflict of all these contradictions shows itself in her face, at once so resolute and so dreamy, so sensual and so intelligent, and beautiful into the bargain with its great coils of hair and the large bright eyes that Southey thought the most expressive he had ever seen. The life of such a woman was bound to be tempestuous. Every day she made theories by which life should be lived; and every day she came smack against the rock of other people's prejudices. Every day too – for she was no pedant, no cold-blooded theorist – something was born in her that thrust aside her theories and forced her to model them afresh. She acted upon her theory that she had no legal claim upon Imlay; she refused to marry him; but when he left her alone week after week with the child she had borne him her agony was unendurable.

Thus distracted, thus puzzling even to herself, the plausible and treacherous Imlay cannot be altogether blamed for failing to follow the rapidity of her changes and the alternate reason and unreason of her moods. Even friends whose liking was impartial were disturbed by her discrepancies. Mary had a passionate, an exuberant, love of Nature, and yet one night when the colours in the sky were so exquisite that Madeleine Schweizer could not help saying to her,

'Come Mary – come, nature-lover – and enjoy this wonderful spectacle – this constant transition from colour to
colour', Mary never took her eyes off the Baron de Wol-
zogen. 'I must confess,' wrote Madame Schweizer, 'that this
erotic absorption made such a disagreeable impression on
me, that all my pleasure vanished.' But if the sentimental
Swiss was disconcerted by Mary's sensuality, Imlay, the
shrewd man of business, was exasperated by her intelligence.
Whenever he saw her he yielded to her charm, but then
her quickness, her penetration, her uncompromising ideal-
ism harassed him. She saw through his excuses; she met all
his reasons; she was even capable of managing his business.
There was no peace with her – he must be off again. And
then her letters followed him, torturing him with their
sincerity and their insight. They were so outspoken; they
pleaded so passionately to be told the truth; they showed
such a contempt for soap and alum and wealth and comfort;
they repeated, as he suspected, so truthfully that he had only
to say the word, 'and you shall never hear of me more', that
he could not endure it. Tickling minnows he had hooked a
dolphin, and the creature rushed him through the waters till
he was dizzy and only wanted to escape. After all, though he
had played at theory-making too, he was a business man, he
depended upon soap and alum; 'the secondary pleasures of
life', he had to admit, 'are very necessary to my comfort'.
And among them was one that for ever evaded Mary's
jealous scrutiny. Was it business, was it politics, was it a
woman, that perpetually took him away from her? He
shillied and shallied; he was very charming when they met;
then he disappeared again. Exasperated at last, and half
insane with suspicion, she forced the truth from the cook. A
little actress in a strolling company was his mistress, she
learnt. True to her own creed of decisive action, Mary at
once soaked her skirts so that she might sink unfailingly,
and threw herself from Putney Bridge. But she was rescued;
after unspeakable agony she recovered, and then her
'unconquerable greatness of mind', her girlish creed of

independence, asserted itself again, and she determined to make another bid for happiness and to earn her living without taking a penny from Imlay for herself or their child.

It was in this crisis that she again saw Godwin, the little man with the big head, whom she had met when the French Revolution was making the young men in Somers Town think that a new world was being born. She met him – but that is a euphemism, for in fact Mary Wollstonecraft actually visited him in his own house. Was it the effect of the French Revolution? Was it the blood she had seen spilt on the pavement and the cries of the furious crowd that had rung in her ears that made it seem a matter of no importance whether she put on her cloak and went to visit Godwin in Somers Town, or waited in Judd Street West for Godwin to come to her? And what strange upheaval of human life was it that inspired that curious man, who was so queer a mixture of meanness and magnanimity, of coldness and deep feeling – for the memoir of his wife could not have been written without unusual depth of heart – to hold the view that she did right – that he respected Mary for trampling upon the idiotic convention by which women's lives were tied down? He held the most extraordinary views on many subjects, and upon the relations of the sexes in particular. He thought that reason should influence even the love between men and women. He thought that there was something spiritual in their relationship. He had written that 'marriage is a law, and the worst of all laws . . . marriage is an affair of property, and the worst of all properties'. He held the belief that if two people of the opposite sex like each other, they should live together without any ceremony, or, for living together is apt to blunt love, twenty doors off, say, in the same street. And he went further; he said that if another man liked your wife 'this will create no difficulty. We may all enjoy her conversation, and we shall all be wise enough to consider the sensual intercourse a very trivial object.' True, when he wrote those words he had never been in love; now for the first time he was to experience that sensation. It came very quietly and naturally, growing 'with equal advances in the mind of each' from those talks in Somers Town, from those discussions upon everything under the sun which they held so improperly alone in his rooms. 'It was friendship melting into love . . .', he wrote. 'When, in the course of things, the disclosure came, there was nothing in a manner for either party to disclose to the other.' Certainly they were in agreement upon the most essential points; they were both of opinion, for instance, that marriage was unnecessary. They would continue to live apart. Only when Nature again intervened, and Mary found herself with child, was it worth while to lose valued friends, she asked, for the sake of a theory? She thought not, and they were married. And then that other theory – that it is best for husband and wife to live apart – was not that also incompatible with other feelings that were coming to birth in her? 'A husband is a convenient part of the furniture of the house', she wrote. Indeed, she discovered that she was passionately domestic. Why not, then, revise that theory too, and share the same roof. Godwin should have a room some doors off to work in; and they should dine out separately if they liked – their work, their friends, should be separate. Thus they settled it, and the plan worked admirably. The arrangement combined 'the novelty and lively sensation of a visit with the more delicious and heart-felt pleasures of domestic life'. Mary admitted that she was happy; Godwin confessed that, after all one's philosophy, it was 'extremely gratifying' to find that 'there is someone who takes an interest in one's happiness'. All sorts of powers and emotions were liberated in Mary by her new satisfaction. Trifles gave her an exquisite pleasure – the sight of Godwin and Imlay's child playing together; the thought of their own child who was to be born; a day's jaunt into the country. One day, meeting Imlay in the New Road, she greeted him without bitterness. But, as Godwin wrote, 'Ours is not an idle happiness, a paradise of selfish and transitory pleasures.' No, it too was an experiment, as Mary's life had been an experiment from the start, an attempt to make human conventions conform more closely to human needs. And their marriage was only a beginning; all sorts of things were to follow after. Mary was going to have a child. She was going to write a book to be called *The Wrongs of Women*. She was going to reform education. She was going to come down to dinner the day after her child was born. She was going to employ a midwife and not a doctor at her confinement – but that experiment was her last. She died in child-birth. She whose sense of her own existence was so intense, who had cried out even in her misery, 'I cannot bear to think of being no more – of losing myself – nay, it appears to me impossible that I should cease to exist', died at the age of thirty-six. But she has her revenge. Many millions have died and been forgotten in the hundred and thirty years that have passed since she was buried; and yet as we read her letters and listen to her arguments and consider her experiments, above all, that most fruitful experiment, her relation with Godwin, and realize the high-handed and hot-blooded manner in which she cut her way to the quick of life, one form of immortality is hers undoubtedly: she is alive and active, she argues and experiments, we hear her voice and trace her influence even now among the living.

Jane Austen Practising

Jane Austen (1775–1817)
This review of Jane Austen's *Love and Freindship*
(now reprinted by The Women's Press, 1978)
appeared in the *New Statesman* on 15 July 1922.

The summer of 1922, remarkable for public
reasons in many ways, was privately remarkable for the
extreme coldness of its nights. Six blankets and a quilt? A
rug and a hot water bottle? All over England men and
women went to bed with such words upon their lips. And
then, between two and three in the morning, they woke
with a start. Something serious had happened. It was stifl-
ing. It was portentous. Steps must be taken immediately.
But what a frightful effort it needs in the early hours of the
morning to throw off all one's clothes!

All over England for the past ten or twenty years the
reputation of Jane Austen has been accumulating on top of
us like these same quilts and blankets. The voices of the
elderly and distinguished, of the clergy and the squirearchy,
have droned in unison praising and petting, capping quota-
tions, telling little anecdotes, raking up little facts. She is
the most perfect artist in English literature. And one of
her cousins had his head cut off in the French Revolution.

Did she ever go fox hunting? No, but she nursed Miss Gibson through the measles. Her knowledge of the upper middle classes was unrivalled. One of her ancestors entertained King Charles. Macaulay, of course, compared her with Shakespeare. And where is Mansfield Park? So they pile up the quilts and counterpanes until the comfort becomes oppressive. Something must be done about it. But what a frightful effort it needs at this time of day to shake off all these clothes!

Now opportunely, in the nick of time, comes *Love and Freindship* to give us the very chance we want. Here is a little book written by Jane Austen long before she was the great Jane Austen of mythology. The Jane Austen of *Love and Freindship* was a girl of seventeen scribbling stories to amuse the schoolroom. One is dedicated with mock solemnity to her brother. Another is nearly illustrated with water-colour heads by her sister. Nobody (for we may leave Mr Chesterton to the end) has been here before us, and so we may really read Jane Austen by ourselves for the first time.

She is a girl of seventeen writing in a country parsonage. And on page two, without turning a hair, out she raps 'natural daughter'. Yet her mother might have come in at that very moment. The eighteenth century, of course, still persisted. The little Austens had the freedom of the house as no other children were to have it for a century at least. Money and marriage would no doubt be jokes in the nursery as they were, much more coarsely, jokes upon the stage. And clever children, beginning to laugh at their elders, would in the year 1790 pick up the last new novel and make fun of its heroine. 'Ah! what could we do but what we did? We sighed and fainted on the sofa.' When Jane Austen read that aloud, no doubt her brothers and sisters took the reference to Adeline Barrett, or whoever was the fashionable heroine of the moment. And as the Austens were a large family, and Mrs Austen stitched and darned and lay an invalid on the sofa, her daughters, while still very young, were well aware that life in a country parsonage has little in common with life in Mrs Radcliffe's novels. This is all plausible enough, and much more might be written in the same strain. But it has nothing whatever to do with *Love and Freindship*. For this girl of seventeen is not writing to amuse the schoolroom. She is not writing to draw a laugh from sister and brothers. She is writing for everybody, for nobody, for our age, for her own; she, in short, is writing. 'A sensibility too trembl-ingly alive to every affliction of my Friends, my Acquaint-ance, and particularly to every affliction of my own, was my only fault, if a fault it could be called. Alas! how altered now! Tho' indeed my own Misfortunes do not make less impression on me than they ever did, yet now I never feel for those of an other.' The authoress of those lines had, if not a whole sitting room to herself, some private corner of the common parlour where she was allowed to write without interruption. But now and then, as the writing of *Love and Freindship* proceeded, a brother or a sister must have asked her what she was laughing at. And then Jane Austen read aloud, 'I die a martyr to my grief for the loss of Augustus. One fatal swoon has cost me my life. Beware of Swoons, Dear Laura. . . . Run mad as often as you chuse, but do not faint. . . .' And taking up her pen again she wrote, it is clear, as fast as she could write, and faster than she could spell, for the incredible adventures of Laura and Sophia popped into her head as quick as lightning. She was in the enviable position of having one page to fill and a bubbling fancy capable of filling half a dozen. So if she wants to dispose of the husband of Phillipa she decrees that he shall have one talent, driving, and one possession, a coach, and he shall drive for ever between Edinburgh and Stirling, or, for Jane Austen does not exaggerate, shall drive to Stirling every other day. And Philander and Gustavus – what shall we do with them? Oh, their mothers (and, by the way, no one knew who their fathers were – perhaps Philip Jones the bricklayer, and Gregory Staves the staymaker) – their mothers kept their fortune of nine hundred pounds in the table drawer. So they stole it, and wrapped it in nine parcels, and spent it in seven weeks and a day, and came home and found their mothers starved, and went upon the stage and acted Macbeth. Spirited, easy, full of fun, verging with freedom upon sheer nonsense, there can be no doubt that *Love and Freindship* makes excellent reading. But what is this note which never merges in the rest, which sounds distinctly and penetratingly all through the volume? It is the sound of laughter. The girl of seventeen is laughing, in her corner, at the world.

Girls of seventeen are always laughing. They laugh when Mr Binney helps himself to salt instead of sugar. They almost die of laughing when old Mrs Tomkins sits down upon the cat. But they are crying the moment after. They have no fixed point from which they see that there is something eternally laughable in human nature. They do not know that wherever they go and however long they live they will always find Lady Grevilles snubbing poor Marias at a dance. But Jane Austen knew it. That is one reason why she is so impersonal and remains for ever so inscrutable. One of those fairies who are said to attend with their gifts upon cradles must have taken her on a flight through the air directly she was born. And when she was laid in her cradle again she knew what the world looked like. She had chosen her kingdom. She had agreed that if she might rule over that territory she would covet no other. Thus at seventeen she had few illusions about other people and none about herself. Whatever she writes is finished and turned and set in its relation to the universe like a work of art. When Jane Austen, the writer, wrote down, in the most remarkable sketch in the book, a little of Lady Greville's conversation, there is no trace of anger at the snub which Jane Austen, the clergyman's daughter, no doubt once received. Her gaze passes straight to the mark, and somehow we know precisely where, upon the map of human nature, that mark is. We know because Jane Austen kept to her compact; she never trespassed beyond her boundaries. Never, even at the emotional age of seventeen, did she round upon herself in shame, and obliterate a sarcasm in a spasm of compassion, or blur an outline in a mist of rhapsody. Spasms and rhapsodies, she seems to have said, end here. And the boundary line is perfectly distinct. But she does not deny that moons and mountains and castles exist – on the other side. She has even one romance of her own. It is for the Queen of Scots. She really admired her very much. 'One of the first characters in the World,' she called her, 'a bewitching Princess whose only freind was then the Duke of Norfolk, and whose only ones now Mr Whitaker, Mrs Lefroy, Mrs Knight and myself.' With these words the passion is neatly circumscribed, and rounded with a laugh. It is amusing to remember how the young Brontës wrote, not so very much later, about the Duke of Wellington.

It may be that we are reading too much into these scraps and scribbles. We are still under the influence of the quilts and counterpanes. But just as we determine to shake ourselves free – and, after all, she was a limited, tart, rather conventional woman for all her genius – we hear a snatch of music. 'Yet truth being I think very excusable in an historian.' And again, 'She was nothing more than a mere good tempered, civil, and obliging young woman; as such we could scarcely dislike her – she was only an object of contempt.' And yet again, '. . . for what could be expected from a man who possessed not the smallest atom of sensibility, who scarcely knew the meaning of simpathy, and who actually snored'. She is only humming a tune beneath her breath, trying over a few bars of the music for *Pride and Prejudice* and *Emma*. But we know that there is no one else who can sing like that. She need not raise her voice. Every syllable comes quite distinctly through the gates of time. And whatever they may say about her genius and her cousins and *Mansfield Park* we are content to listen all day long to Jane Austen practising.

Jane Austen

This essay, published in *The Common Reader: First Series*, incorporates a revision of 'Jane Austen Practising' as well as material from a review of *The Works of Jane Austen* which appeared in the *Nation and Athenaeum* on 15 December 1923. Virginia Woolf also reviewed works by or about Jane Austen in *The Times Literary Supplement*, 28 October 1920 and 20 July 1922.

It is probable that if Miss Cassandra Austen had had her way we should have had nothing of Jane Austen's except her novels. To her elder sister alone did she write freely; to her alone she confided her hopes and, if rumour is true, the one great disappointment of her life; but when Miss Cassandra Austen grew old, and the growth of her sister's fame made her suspect that a time might come when strangers would pry and scholars speculate, she burnt, at great cost to herself, every letter that could gratify their curiosity, and spared only what she judged too trivial to be of interest.

Hence our knowledge of Jane Austen is derived from a little gossip, a few letters, and her books. As for the gossip, gossip which has survived its day is never despicable; with a little rearrangement it suits our purpose admirably. For example, Jane 'is not at all pretty and very prim, unlike a girl of twelve . . . Jane is whimsical and affected', says little Philadelphia Austen of her cousin. Then we have Mrs

Mitford, who knew the Austens as girls and thought Jane 'the prettiest, silliest, most affected husband-hunting butterfly she ever remembers'. Next, there is Miss Mitford's anonymous friend 'who visits her now [and] says that she has stiffened into the most perpendicular, precise, taciturn piece of "single blessedness" that ever existed, and that, until *Pride and Prejudice* showed what a precious gem was hidden in that unbending case, she was no more regarded in society than a poker or firescreen. . . . The case is very different now', the good lady goes on; 'she is still a poker – but a poker of whom everybody is afraid. . . . A wit, a delineator of character, who does not talk is terrific indeed!' On the other side, of course, there are the Austens, a race little given to panegyric of themselves, but nevertheless, they say, her brothers, 'were very fond and very proud of her. They were attached to her by her talents, her virtues, and her engaging manners, and each loved afterwards to fancy a resemblance in some niece or daughter of his own to the dear sister Jane, whose perfect equal they yet never expected to see.' Charming but perpendicular, loved at home but feared by strangers, biting of tongue but tender of heart – these contrasts are by no means incompatible, and when we turn to the novels we shall find ourselves stumbling there too over the same complexities in the writer.

To begin with, that prim little girl whom Philadelphia found so unlike a child of twelve, whimsical and affected, was soon to be the authoress of an astonishing and unchildish story, *Love and Freindship,* which, incredible though it appears, was written at the age of fifteen. It was written, apparently, to amuse the schoolroom; one of the stories in the same book is dedicated with mock solemnity to her brother; another is neatly illustrated with water-colour heads by her sister. These are jokes which, one feels, were family property; thrusts of satire, which went home because all little Austens made mock in common of fine ladies who 'sighed and fainted on the sofa'.

Brothers and sisters must have laughed when Jane read

out loud her last hit at the vices which they all abhorred. 'I die a martyr to my grief for the loss of Augustus. One fatal swoon has cost me my life. Beware of Swoons, Dear Laura. . . . Run mad as often as you chuse, but do not faint. . . .' And on she rushed, as fast as she could write and quicker than she could spell, to tell the incredible adventures of Laura and Sophia, of Philander and Gustavus, of the gentleman who drove a coach between Edinburgh and Stirling every other day, of the theft of the fortune that was kept in the table drawer, of the starving mothers and the sons who acted Macbeth. Undoubtedly, the story must have roused the schoolroom to uproarious laughter. And yet, nothing is more obvious than that this girl of fifteen, sitting in her private corner of the common parlour, was writing not to draw a laugh from brother and sisters, and not for home consumption. She was writing for everybody, for nobody, for our age, for her own; in other words, even at that early age Jane Austen was writing. One hears it in the rhythm and shapeliness and severity of the sentences. 'She was nothing more than a mere good-tempered, civil, and obliging young woman; as such we could scarcely dislike her – she was only an object of contempt.' Such a sentence is meant to outlast the Christmas holidays. Spirited, easy, full of fun, verging with freedom upon sheer non-sense – *Love and Freindship* is all that; but what is this note which never merges in the rest, which sounds distinctly and penetratingly all through the volume? It is the sound of laughter. The girl of fifteen is laughing, in her corner, at the world.

Girls of fifteen are always laughing. They laugh when Mr Binney helps himself to salt instead of sugar. They almost die of laughing when old Mrs Tomkins sits down upon the cat. But they are crying the moment after. They have no fixed abode from which they see that there is something eternally laughable in human nature, some quality in men and women that for ever excites our satire. They do not know that Lady Greville who snubs, and poor Maria who is

111

snubbed, are permanent features of every ballroom. But Jane Austen knew it from her birth upwards. One of those fairies who perch upon cradles must have taken her on a flight through the world directly she was born. When she was laid in the cradle again she knew not only what the world looked like, but had already chosen her kingdom. She had agreed that if she might rule over that territory, she would covet no other. Thus at fifteen she had few illusions about other people and none about herself. Whatever she writes is finished and turned and set in its relation, not to the parsonage, but to the universe. She is impersonal; she is inscrutable. When the writer, Jane Austen, wrote down in the most remarkable sketch in the book a little of Lady Greville's conversation, there is no trace of anger at the snub which the clergyman's daughter, Jane Austen, once received. Her gaze passes straight to the mark, and we know precisely where, upon the map of human nature, that mark is. We know because Jane Austen kept to her compact; she never trespassed beyond her boundaries. Never, even at the emotional age of fifteen, did she round upon herself in shame, obliterate a sarcasm in a spasm of compassion, or blur an outline in a mist of rhapsody. Spasms and rhapsodies, she seems to have said, pointing with her stick, end *there*; and the boundary line is perfectly distinct. But she does not deny that moons and mountains and castles exist – on the other side. She has even one romance of her own. It is for the Queen of Scots. She really admired her very much. 'One of the first characters in the world,' she called her, 'a bewitching Princess whose only friend was then the Duke of Norfolk, and whose only ones now Mr Whitaker, Mrs Lefroy, Mrs Knight and myself.' With these words her passion is neatly circumscribed, and rounded with a laugh. It is amusing to remember in what terms the young Brontës wrote, not very much later, in their northern parsonage, about the Duke of Wellington.

The prim little girl grew up. She became 'the prettiest, silliest, most affected husband-hunting butterfly, Mrs

Mitford ever remembered, and, incidentally, the authoress of a novel called *Pride and Prejudice*, which, written stealthily under cover of a creaking door, lay for many years unpublished. A little later, it is thought, she began another story, *The Watsons*, and being for some reason dissatisfied with it, left it unfinished. The second-rate works of a great writer are worth reading because they offer the best criticism of his masterpieces. Here her difficulties are more apparent, and the method she took to overcome them less artfully concealed. To begin with, the stiffness and the bareness of the first chapters prove that she was one of those writers who lay their facts out rather baldly in the first version and then go back and back and back and cover them with flesh and atmosphere. How it would have been done we cannot say – by what suppressions and insertions and artful devices. But the miracle would have been accomplished; the dull history of fourteen years of family life would have been converted into another of those exquisite and apparently effortless introductions; and we should never have guessed what pages of preliminary drudgery Jane Austen forced her pen to go through. Here we perceive that she was no conjuror after all. Like other writers, she had to create the atmosphere in which her own peculiar genius could bear fruit. Here she fumbles; here she keeps us waiting. Suddenly she has done it; now things can happen as she likes things to happen. The Edwardses are going to the ball. The Tomlinsons' carriage is passing; she can tell us that Charles is 'being provided with his gloves and told to keep them on'; Tom Musgrave retreats to a remote corner with a barrel of oysters and is famously snug. Her genius is freed and active. At once our senses quicken; we are possessed with the peculiar intensity which she alone can impart. But of what is it all composed? Of a ball in a country town; a few couples meeting and taking hands in an assembly room; a little eating and drinking; and for catastrophe, a boy being snubbed by one young lady and kindly treated by another. There is no tragedy and no heroism. Yet for some reason the little

113

scene is moving out of all proportion to its surface solemnity. We have been made to see that if Emma acted so in the ball-room, how considerate, how tender, inspired by what sincerity of feeling she would have shown herself in those graver crises of life which, as we watch her, come inevitably before our eyes. Jane Austen is thus a mistress of much deeper emotion than appears upon the surface. She stimulates us to supply what is not there. What she offers is, apparently, a trifle, yet is composed of something that expands in the reader's mind and endows with the most enduring form of life scenes which are outwardly trivial. Always the stress is laid upon character. How, we are made to wonder, will Emma behave when Lord Osborne and Tom Musgrave make their call at five minutes before three, just as Mary is bringing in the tray and the knife-case? It is an extremely awkward situation. The young men are accustomed to much greater refinement. Emma may prove herself ill-bred, vulgar, a nonentity. The turns and twists of the dialogue keep us on the tenterhooks of suspense. Our attention is half upon the present moment, half upon the future. And when, in the end, Emma behaves in such a way as to vindicate our highest hopes of her, we are moved as if we had been made witnesses of a matter of the highest importance. Here, indeed, in this unfinished and in the main inferior story, are all the elements of Jane Austen's greatness. It has the permanent quality of literature. Think away the surface animation, the likeness to life, and there remains, to provide a deeper pleasure, an exquisite discrimination of human values. Dismiss this too from the mind and one can dwell with extreme satisfaction upon the more abstract art which, in the ball-room scene, so varies the emotions and proportions the parts that it is possible to enjoy it, as one enjoys poetry, for itself, and not as a link which carries the story this way and that.

But the gossip says of Jane Austen that she was perpendicular, precise, and taciturn – 'a poker of whom everybody is afraid'. Of this too there are traces; she could be merciless enough; she is one of the most consistent satirists in the whole of literature. Those first angular chapters of *The Watsons* prove that hers was not a prolific genius; she had not, like Emily Brontë, merely to open the door to make herself felt. Humbly and gaily she collected the twigs and straws out of which the nest was to be made and placed them neatly together. The twigs and straws were a little dry and a little dusty in themselves. There was the big house and the little house; a tea party, a dinner party, and an occasional picnic; life was hedged in by valuable connections and adequate incomes; by muddy roads, wet feet, and a tendency on the part of the ladies to get tired; a little principle supported it, a little consequence, and the education commonly enjoyed by upper middle-class families living in the country. Vice, adventure, passion were left outside. But of all this prosiness, of all this littleness, she evades nothing, and nothing is slurred over. Patiently and precisely she tells us how they 'made no stop anywhere till they reached Newbury, where a comfortable meal, uniting dinner and supper, wound up the enjoyments and fatigues of the day'. Nor does she pay to conventions merely the tribute of lip homage; she believes in them besides accepting them. When she is describing a clergyman, like Edmund Bertram, or a sailor, in particular, she appears debarred by the sanctity of his office from the free use of her chief tool, the comic genius, and is apt therefore to lapse into decorous panegyric or matter-of-fact description. But these are exceptions; for the most part her attitude recalls the anonymous lady's ejaculation – 'A wit, a delineator of character, who does not talk is terrific indeed!' She wishes neither to reform nor to annihilate; she is silent; and that is terrific indeed. One after another she creates her fools, her prigs, her worldlings, her Mr Collinses, her Sir Walter Elliotts, her Mrs Bennets. She encircles them with the lash of a whip-like phrase which, as it runs round them, cuts out their silhouettes for ever. But there they remain; no excuse is found for them and no mercy shown them. Nothing remains of Julia and Maria Bertram when she has done with them; Lady Bertram is left 'sitting and calling to Pug and trying to keep him from the flower-beds' eternally. A divine justice is meted out; Dr Grant, who begins by liking his goose tender, ends by bringing on 'apoplexy and death, by three great institutionary dinners in one week'. Sometimes it seems as if her creatures were born merely to give Jane Austen the supreme delight of slicing their heads off. She is satisfied; she is content; she would not alter a hair on anybody's head, or move one brick or one blade of grass in a world which provides her with such exquisite delight.

Nor, indeed, would we. For even if the pangs of outraged vanity, or the heat of moral wrath, urged us to improve away a world so full of spite, pettiness, and folly, the task is beyond our powers. People are like that – the girl of fifteen knew it; the mature woman proves it. At this very moment some Lady Bertram is trying to keep Pug from the flower beds; she sends Chapman to help Miss Fanny a little late. The discrimination is so perfect, the satire so just, that, consistent though it is, it almost escapes our notice. No touch of pettiness, no hint of spite, rouse us from our contemplation. Delight strangely mingles with our amusement. Beauty illumines these fools.

That elusive quality is, indeed, often made up of very different parts, which it needs a peculiar genius to bring together. The wit of Jane Austen has for partner the perfection of her taste. Her fool is a fool, her snob is a snob, because he departs from the model of sanity and sense which she has in mind, and conveys to us unmistakably even while she makes us laugh. Never did any novelist make more use of an impeccable sense of human values. It is against the disc of an unerring heart, an unfailing good taste, an almost stern morality, that she shows up those deviations from kindness, truth, and sincerity which are among the most delightful things in English literature. She depicts a Mary Crawford in her mixture of good and bad entirely by this means. She lets her rattle on against the clergy, or in favour of a baronetage and ten thousand a year, with all the ease and spirit possible; but now and again she strikes one note of her own, very quietly, but in perfect tune, and at once all Mary Crawford's chatter, though it continues to amuse, rings flat. Hence the depth, the beauty, the complexity of her scenes. From such contrasts there comes a beauty, a solemnity even, which are not only as remarkable as her wit, but an inseparable part of it. In *The Watsons* she gives us a foretaste of this power; she makes us wonder why an ordinary act of kindness, as she describes it, becomes so full of meaning. In her master-pieces, the same gift is brought to perfection. Here is nothing out of the way; it is midday in Northamptonshire; a dull young man is talking to rather a weakly young woman on the stairs as they go up to dress for dinner, with house-maids passing. But, from triviality, from commonplace, their words become suddenly full of meaning, and the moment for both one of the most memorable in their lives. It fills itself; it shines; it glows; it hangs before us, deep, trembling, serene for a second; next, the housemaid passes, and this drop, in which all the happiness of life has collected, gently subsides again to become part of the ebb and flow of ordinary existence.

What more natural, then, with this insight into their profundity, than that Jane Austen should have chosen to write of the trivialities of day-to-day existence, of parties, picnics, and country dances? No 'suggestions to alter her style of writing' from the Prince Regent or Mr Clarke could tempt her; no romance, no adventure, no politics or intrigue could hold a candle to life on a country-house staircase as she saw it. Indeed, the Prince Regent and his librarian had run their heads against a very formidable obstacle; they were trying to tamper with an incorruptible conscience, to disturb an infallible discretion. The child who formed her sentences so finely when she was fifteen never ceased to form them, and never wrote for the Prince Regent or his Librarian, but for the world at large. She knew exactly what her powers were, and what material they were fitted to deal with as material should be dealt with by a writer whose standard of finality was high. There were impressions that lay outside her province; emotions that by no stretch or artifice could be properly coated and covered by her own resources. For example, she could not make a girl talk enthusiastically of banners and chapels. She could not throw herself whole-heartedly into a romantic moment. She had all sorts of devices for evading scenes of passion. Nature and its beauties she approached in a sidelong way of her own. She describes a beautiful night without once mentioning the moon. Nevertheless, as we read the few formal phrases about 'the brilliancy of an unclouded night and the contrast of the deep shade of the woods', the night is at once as 'solemn, and soothing, and lovely' as she tells us, quite simply, that it was.

The balance of her gifts was singularly perfect. Among her finished novels there are no failures, and among her many chapters few that sink markedly below the level of the others. But, after all, she died at the age of forty-two. She died at the height of her powers. She was still subject to those changes which often make the final period of a writer's career the most interesting of all. Vivacious, irrepressible, gifted with an invention of great vitality, there can be no doubt that she would have written more, had she lived, and it is tempting to consider whether she would not have written differently. The boundaries were marked; moons, mountains, and castles lay on the other side. But was she not sometimes tempted to trespass for a minute? Was she not beginning, in her own gay and brilliant manner, to contemplate a little voyage of discovery?

Let us take *Persuasion*, the last competed novel, and look by its light at the books she might have written had she lived. There is a peculiar beauty and a peculiar dullness in *Persuasion*. The dullness is that which so often marks the transition stage between two different periods. The writer is a little bored. She has grown too familiar with the ways of her world; she no longer notes them freshly. There is an asperity in her comedy which suggests that she has almost ceased to be amused by the vanities of a Sir Walter or the snobbery of a Miss Elliott. The satire is harsh, and the comedy crude. She is no longer so freshly aware of the amusements of daily life. Her mind is not altogether on her object. But, while we feel that Jane Austen has done this before, and done it better, we also feel that she is trying to do something which she has never yet attempted. There is a new element in *Persuasion*, the quality, perhaps, that made Dr Whewell fire up and insist that it was 'the most beautiful of her works'. She is beginning to discover that the world is larger, more mysterious, and more romantic than she had supposed. We feel it to be true of herself when she says of Anne: 'She had been forced into prudence in her youth, she learned romance as she grew older – the natural sequel of an unnatural beginning.' She dwells frequently upon the beauty and the melancholy of nature, upon the autumn where she had been wont to dwell upon the spring. She talks of the 'influence so sweet and so sad of autumnal months in the country'. She marks 'the tawny leaves and withered hedges'. 'One does not love a place the less because one has suffered in it', she observes. But it is not only in a new sensibility to nature that we detect the change. Her attitude to life itself is altered. She is seeing it, for the greater part of the book, through the eyes of a woman who, unhappy herself, has a special sympathy for the happiness and unhappiness of others, which, until the very end, she is forced to comment upon in silence. Therefore the observation is less of facts and more of feelings than is usual. There is an expressed emotion in the scene at the concert and in the famous talk about woman's constancy which proves not merely the biographical fact that Jane Austen had loved, but the aesthetic fact that she was no longer afraid to say so. Experience, when it was of a serious kind, had to sink very deep, and to be thoroughly disinfected by the passage of time, before she allowed herself to deal with it in fiction. But now, in 1817, she was ready. Outwardly, too, in her circumstances, a change was imminent. Her fame had grown very slowly. 'I doubt', wrote Mr Austen Leigh, 'whether it would be possible to mention any other author of note whose personal obscurity was so complete.' Had she lived a few more years only, all that would have been altered. She would have stayed in London, dined out, lunched out, met famous people, made new friends, read, travelled, and carried back to the quiet country cottage a hoard of observations to feast upon at leisure.

And what effect would all this have had upon the six novels that Jane Austen did not write? She would not have written of crime, of passion, or of adventure. She would not have been rushed by the importunity of publishers or the flattery of friends into slovenliness or insincerity. But she would have been shaken. Her comedy would have suffered. She would have trusted less (this is already perceptible in *Persuasion*) to dialogue and more to reflection to give us a knowledge of her characters. Those marvellous little speeches which sum up, in a few minutes' chatter, all that we need in order to know an Admiral Croft or a Mrs Musgrove for ever, that shorthand, hit-or-miss method which contains chapters of analysis and psychology, would have become too crude to hold all that she now perceived of the complexity of human nature. She would have devised a method, clear and composed as ever, but deeper and more suggestive, for conveying not only what people say, but what they leave unsaid; not only what they are, but what life is. She would have stood farther away from her characters, and seen them more as a group, less as individuals. Her satire, while it played less incessantly, would have been more stringent and severe. She would have been the forerunner of Henry James and of Proust – but enough. Vain are these speculations: the most perfect artist among women, the writer whose books are immortal, died 'just as she was beginning to feel confidence in her own success'.

Haworth, November 1904

This description of a pilgrimage to Haworth was,
fittingly, Virginia Woolf's first work to be
accepted for publication (although in fact the second to appear in print). It was published in *The
Guardian* (a weekly), unsigned, on 21 December
1904. It is reprinted in *Books and Portraits*.

I do not know whether pilgrimages to the shrines
of famous men ought not to be condemned as sentimental
journeys. It is better to read Carlyle in your own study chair
than to visit the sound-proof room and pore over the manuscripts at Chelsea. I should be inclined to set an examination
on Frederick the Great in place of entrance fee; only, in that
case, the house would soon have to be shut up. The curiosity
is only legitimate when the house of a great writer or the
country in which it is set adds something to our understanding of his books. This justification you have for a pilgrimage
to the home and country of Charlotte Brontë and her sisters.
The *Life*, by Mrs Gaskell, gives you the impression
that Haworth and the Brontës are somehow inextricably
mixed. Haworth expresses the Brontës; the Brontës express
Haworth; they fit like a snail to its shell. How far surround-
ings radically affect people's minds, it is not for me to ask:
superfically, the influence is great, but it is worth asking if
the famous parsonage had been placed in a London slum,

the dens of Whitechapel would not have had the same result as the lonely Yorkshire moors. However, I am taking away my only excuse for visiting Haworth. Unreasonable or not, one of the chief points of a recent visit to Yorkshire was that an expedition to Haworth could be accomplished. The necessary arrangements were made, and we determined to take advantage of the first day for our expedition. A real northern snowstorm had been doing the honours of the moors. It was rash to wait fine weather, and it was also cowardly. I understand that the sun very seldom shone on the Brontë family, and if we chose a really fine day we should have to make allowance for the fact that fifty years ago there were few fine days at Haworth, and that we were, therefore, for sake of comfort, rubbing out half the shadows in the picture. However, it would be interesting to see what impression Haworth could make upon the brilliant weather of Settle. We certainly passed through a very cheerful land, which might be likened to a vast wedding cake, of which the icing was slightly undulating; the earth was bridal in its virgin snow, which helped to suggest the comparison.

Keighley – pronounced Keethly – is often mentioned in the *Life*; it was the big town four miles from Haworth in which Charlotte walked to make her more important purchases – her wedding gown, perhaps, and the thin little cloth boots which we examined under glass in the Brontë Museum. It is a big manufacturing town, hard and stony, and clattering with business, in the way of these Northern towns. They make small provision for the sentimental traveller, and our only occupation was to picture the slight figure of Charlotte trotting along the streets in her thin mantle, hustled into the gutter by more burly passers-by. It was the Keighley of her day, and that was some comfort. Our excitement as we neared Haworth had in it an element of suspense that was really painful, as though we were to meet some long-separated friend, who might have changed in the interval – so clear an image of Haworth had we from print and picture. At a certain point we entered the valley, up both sides of which the village climbs, and right on the hill-top, looking down over its parish, we saw the famous oblong tower of the church. This marked the shrine at which we were to do homage.

It may have been the effect of a sympathetic imagination, but I think that there were good reasons why Haworth did certainly strike one not exactly as gloomy, but, what is worse for artistic purposes, as dingy and commonplace. The houses, built of yellow-brown stone, date from the early nineteenth century. They climb the moor step by step in little detached strips, some distance apart, so that the town instead of making one compact blot on the landscape has contrived to get a whole stretch into its clutches. There is a long line of houses up the moor-side, which clusters round the church and parsonage with a little clump of trees. At the top the interest for a Brontë lover becomes suddenly intense. The church, the parsonage, the Brontë Museum, the school where Charlotte taught, and the Bull Inn where Branwell drank are all within a stone's throw of each other. The museum is certainly rather a pallid and inanimate collection of objects. An effort ought to be made to keep things out of these mausoleums, but the choice often lies between them and destruction, so that we must be grateful for the care which has preserved much that is, under any circumstances, of deep interest. Here are many autograph letters, pencil drawings, and other documents. But the most touching case – so touching that one hardly feels reverent in one's gaze – is that which contains the little personal relics, the dresses and shoes of the dead woman. The natural fate of such things is to die before the body that wore them, and because these, trifling and transient though they are, have survived, Charlotte Brontë the woman comes to life, and one forgets the chiefly memorable fact that she was a great writer. Her shoes and her thin muslin dress have outlived her. One other object gives a thrill; the little oak stool which Emily carried with her on her solitary moorland tramps, and on which she sat, if not to write, as they say, to think what was probably better than her writing.

The church, of course, save part of the tower, is renewed since Brontë days; but that remarkable churchyard remains. The old edition of the *Life* had on its title-page a little print which struck the keynote of the book; it seemed to be all graves – gravestones stood ranked all round; you walked on a pavement lettered with dead names; the graves had solemnly invaded the garden of the parsonage itself, which was as a little oasis of life in the midst of the dead. This is no exaggeration of the artist's, as we found: the stones seem to start out of the ground at you in tall, upright lines, like an army of silent soldiers. There is no hand's breadth untenanted; indeed, the economy of space is somewhat irreverent. In old days a flagged path, which suggested the slabs of graves, led from the front door of the parsonage to the churchyard without interruption of wall or hedge; the garden was practically the graveyard too; the successors of the Brontës, however, wishing a little space between life and death, planted a hedge and several tall trees, which now cut off the parsonage garden completely. The house itself is precisely the same as it was in Charlotte's day, save that one new wing has been added. It is easy to shut the eye to this, and then you have the square, boxlike parsonage, built of the ugly, yellow-brown stone which they quarry from the moors behind, precisely as it was when Charlotte lived and died there. Inside, of course, the changes are many, though not such as to obscure the original shape of the rooms. There is nothing remarkable in a mid-Victorian parsonage, though tenanted by genius, and the only room which awakens curiosity is the kitchen, now used as an ante-room, in which the girls tramped as they conceived their work. One other spot has a certain grim interest – the oblong recess beside the staircase into which Emily drove her bulldog during the famous fight, and pinned him while she pommelled him. It is otherwise a little sparse parsonage, much like others of its kind. It was due to the courtesy of the present incumbent that we were allowed to inspect it; in his place I should often feel inclined to exorcise the three famous ghosts.

One thing only remained: the church in which Charlotte worshipped, was married, and lies buried. The circumference of her life was very narrow. Here, though much is altered, a few things remain to tell of her. The slab which bears the names of the succession of children and of their parents – their births and deaths – strikes the eye first. Name follows name; at very short intervals they died – Maria the mother, Maria the daughter, Elizabeth, Branwell, Emily, Anne, Charlotte, and lastly the old father, who outlived them all. Emily was only thirty years old, and Charlotte but nine years older. 'The sting of death is sin, and the strength of sin is the law, but thanks be to God which giveth us the victory through our Lord Jesus Christ.' That is the inscription which has been placed beneath their names, and with reason; for however harsh the struggle, Emily, and Charlotte above all, fought to victory.

'Jane Eyre' and
'Wuthering Heights'

Charlotte Brontë (1816–55) published *Jane Eyre* in 1847, the same year in which Emily Brontë (1818–48) published *Wuthering Heights*
This essay incorporates material from an article on Charlotte Brontë in *The Times Literary Supplement* of 13 April 1916. It was published in *The Common Reader:* First Series. Reviews of works by or about the Brontë sisters also appeared in *The Times Literary Supplement* on 13 December 1917 and 20 July 1922.

Of the hundred years that have passed since Charlotte Brontë was born, she, the centre now of so much legend, devotion, and literature, lived but thirty-nine. It is strange to reflect how different those legends might have been had her life reached the ordinary human span. She might have become, like some of her famous contemporaries, a figure familiarly met with in London and elsewhere, the subject of pictures and anecdotes innumerable, the writer of many novels, of memoirs possibly, removed from us well within the memory of the middle-aged in all the splendour of established fame. She might have been wealthy, she might have been prosperous. But it is not so. When we think of her we have to imagine some one who had no lot in our modern world; we have to cast our minds back to the 'fifties of the last century, to a remote parsonage upon the wild Yorkshire moors. In that parsonage, and on those moors, unhappy and lonely, in her poverty and her exaltation, she remains for ever.

These circumstances, as they affected her character, may have left their traces on her work. A novelist, we reflect, is bound to build up his structure with much very perishable material which begins by lending it reality and ends by cumbering it with rubbish. As we open *Jane Eyre* once more we cannot stifle the suspicion that we shall find her world of imagination as antiquated, mid-Victorian, and out of date as the parsonage on the moor, a place only to be visited by the curious, only preserved by the pious. So we open *Jane Eyre*; and in two pages every doubt is swept clean from our minds.

Folds of scarlet drapery shut in my view to the right hand; to the left were the clear panes of glass, protecting, but not separating me from the drear November day. At intervals, while turning over the leaves of my book, I studied the aspect of that winter afternoon. Afar, it offered a pale blank of mist and cloud; near, a scene of wet lawn and storm-beat shrub, with ceaseless rain sweeping away wildly before a long and lamentable blast.

There is nothing more perishable than the moor itself, or more subject to the sway of fashion than the 'long and lamentable blast'. Nor is this exhilaration short-lived. It rushes us through the entire volume, without giving us time to think, without letting us lift our eyes from the page. So intense is our absorption that if someone moves in the room the movement seems to take place not there but up in Yorkshire. The writer has us by the hand, forces us along her road, makes us see what she sees, never leaves us for a moment or allows us to forget her. At the end we are steeped through and through with the genius, the vehemence, the indignation of Charlotte Brontë. Remarkable faces, figures of strong outline and gnarled feature have flashed upon us in passing; but it is through her eyes that we have seen them. Once she is gone, we seek for them in vain. Think of Rochester and we have to think of Jane Eyre. Think of the moor, and again there is Jane Eyre. Think of the drawing-room,[1] even, those 'white carpets on which seemed laid brilliant garlands of flowers', that 'pale Parian mantelpiece' with its Bohemia glass of 'ruby red' and the 'general blending of snow and fire' – what is all that except Jane Eyre?

The drawbacks of being Jane Eyre are not far to seek. Always to be a governess and always to be in love is a serious limitation in a world which is full, after all, of people who are neither one nor the other. The characters of a Jane Austen or of a Tolstoi have a million facets compared with these. They live and are complex by means of their effect upon many different people who serve to mirror them in the round. They move hither and thither whether their creators watch them or not, and the world in which they live seems to us an independent world which we can visit, now that they have created it, by ourselves. Thomas Hardy is more akin to Charlotte Brontë in the power of his personality and the narrowness of his vision. But the differences are vast. As we read *Jude the Obscure* we are not rushed to a finish; we brood and ponder and drift away from the text in plethoric trains of thought which build up round the characters an atmosphere of question and suggestion of which they are themselves, as often as not, unconscious. Simple peasants as they are, we are forced to confront them with destinies and questionings of the hugest import, so that often it seems as if the most important characters in a Hardy novel are those

[1] Charlotte and Emily Brontë had much the same sense of colour. '. . . we saw – ah! it was beautiful – a splendid place carpeted with crimson, and crimson-covered chairs and tables, and a pure white ceiling bordered by gold, a shower of glass drops hanging in silver chains from the centre, and shimmering with little soft tapers' (*Wuthering Heights*). 'Yet it was merely a very pretty drawing-room, and within it a boudoir, both spread with white carpets, on which seemed laid brilliant garlands of flowers; both ceiled with snowy mouldings of white grapes and vine leaves, beneath which glowed in rich contrast crimson couches and ottomans; while the ornaments on the pale Parian mantelpiece were of sparkling Bohemia glass, ruby red; and between the windows large mirrors repeated the general blending of snow and fire' (*Jane Eyre*).

which have no names. Of this power, of this speculative curiosity, Charlotte Brontë has no trace. She does not attempt to solve the problems of human life; she is even unaware that such problems exist; all her force, and it is the more tremendous for being constricted, goes into the assertion, 'I love', 'I hate', 'I suffer'.

For the self-centred and self-limited writers have a power denied the more catholic and broad-minded. Their impressions are close packed and strongly stamped between their narrow walls. Nothing issues from their minds which has not been marked with their own impress. They learn little from other writers, and what they adopt they cannot assimilate. Both Hardy and Charlotte Brontë appear to have founded their styles upon a stiff and decorous journalism. The staple of their prose is awkward and unyielding. But both with labour and the most obstinate integrity, by thinking every thought until it has subdued words to itself, have forged for themselves a prose which takes the mould of their minds entire; which has, into the bargain, a beauty, a power, a swiftness of its own. Charlotte Brontë, at least, owed nothing to the reading of many books. She never learnt the smoothness of the professional writer, or acquired his ability to stuff and sway his language as he chooses. 'I could never rest in communication with strong, discreet, and refined minds, whether male or female', she writes, as any leader-writer in a provincial journal might have written; but gathering fire and speed goes on in her own authentic voice 'till I had passed the outworks of conventional reserve and crossed the threshold of confidence, and won a place by their hearts' very hearthstone'. It is there that she takes her seat; it is the red and fitful glow of the heart's fire which illumines her page. In other words, we read Charlotte Brontë not for exquisite observation of character – her characters are vigorous and elementary; not for comedy – hers is grim and crude; not for a philosophic view of life – hers is that of a country parson's daughter; but for her poetry. Probably that is so with all writers who have, as she has, an overpowering personality, so that, as we say in real life, they have only to open the door to make themselves felt. There is in them some untamed ferocity perpetually at war with the accepted order of things which makes them desire to create instantly rather than to observe patiently. This very ardour, rejecting half shades and other minor impediments, wings its way past the daily conduct of ordinary people and allies itself with their more inarticulate passions. It makes them poets, or, if they choose to write in prose, intolerant of its restrictions. Hence it is that both Emily and Charlotte are always invoking the help of nature. They both feel the need of some more powerful symbol of the vast and slumbering passions in human nature than words or actions can convey. It is with a description of a storm that Charlotte ends her finest novel *Villette*. 'The skies hang full and dark – a wrack sails from the west; the clouds cast themselves into strange forms.' So she calls in nature to describe a state of mind which could not otherwise be expressed. But neither of the sisters observed nature accurately as Dorothy Wordsworth observed it, or painted it minutely as Tennyson painted it. They seized those aspects of the earth which were most akin to what they themselves felt or imputed to their characters, and so their storms, their moors, their lovely spaces of summer weather are not ornaments applied to decorate a dull page or display the writer's powers of observation – they carry on the emotion and light up the meaning of the book.

The meaning of a book, which lies so often apart from what happens and what is said and consists rather in some connection which things in themselves different have had for the writer, is necessarily hard to grasp. Especially this is so when, like the Brontës, the writer is poetic, and his meaning inseparable from his language, and itself rather a mood than a particular observation. *Wuthering Heights* is a more difficult book to understand than *Jane Eyre*, because Emily was a greater poet than Charlotte. When Charlotte wrote she said with eloquence and splendour and passion 'I love', 'I hate', 'I suffer'. Her experience, though more intense, is on a level with our own. But there is no 'I' in *Wuthering Heights*. There are no governesses. There are no employers. There is love, but it is not the love of men and women. Emily was inspired by some more general conception. The impulse which urged her to create was not her own suffering or her own injuries. She looked out upon a world cleft into gigantic disorder and felt within her the power to unite it in a book. That gigantic ambition is to be felt throughout the novel – a struggle, half thwarted but of superb conviction, to say something through the mouths of her characters which is not merely 'I love' or 'I hate', but 'we, the whole human race' and 'you, the eternal powers . . .' the sentence remains unfinished. It is not strange that it should be so; rather it is astonishing that she can make us feel what she had it in her to say at all. It surges up in the half-articulate words of Catherine Earnshaw, 'If all else perished and *he* remained, I should still continue to be; and if all else remained and he were annihilated, the universe would turn to a mighty stranger; I should not seem part of it'. It breaks out again in the presence of the dead. 'I see a repose that neither earth nor hell can break, and I feel an assurance of the endless and shadowless hereafter – the eternity they have entered – where life is boundless in its duration, and love in its sympathy and joy in its fulness.' It is this suggestion of power underlying the apparitions of human nature and lifting them up into the presence of greatness that gives the book its huge stature among other novels. But it was not enough for Emily Brontë to write a few lyrics, to utter a cry, to express a creed. In her poems she did this once and for all, and her poems will perhaps outlast her novel. But she was novelist as well as poet. She must take upon herself a more laborious and a more ungrateful task. She must face the fact of other existences, grapple with the mechanism of external things, build up, in recognizable shape, farms and houses and report the speeches of men and women who existed independently of herself. And so we reach these summits of emotion not by rant or rhapsody but by hearing a girl sing old songs to herself as she rocks in the branches of a tree; by watching the moor sheep crop the turf; by listening to the soft wind breathing through the grass. The life at the farm with all its absurdities and its improbability is laid open to us. We are given every opportunity of comparing *Wuthering Heights* with a real farm and Heathcliff with a real man. How, we are allowed to ask, can there be truth or insight or the finer shades of emotion in men and women who so little resemble what we have seen ourselves? But even as we ask it we see in Heathcliff the brother that a sister of genius might have seen; he is impossible we say, but nevertheless no boy in literature has a more vivid existence than his. So it is with the two Catherines; never could women feel as they do or act in their manner, we say. All the same, they are the most lovable women in English fiction. It is as if she could tear up all that we know human beings by, and fill these unrecognizable transparences with such a gust of life that they transcend reality. Hers, then, is the rarest of all powers. She could free life from its dependence on facts; with a few touches indicate the spirit of a face so that it needs no body; by speaking of the moor make the wind blow and the thunder roar.

'Aurora Leigh'

Elizabeth Barrett Browning (1806–61) published
Aurora Leigh in 1857. (The poem is now
reprinted, with an introduction by Cora Kaplan,
by The Women's Press, 1978)
This essay appeared in *The Common Reader:*
Second Series, based on articles in *Yale Review*,
June 1931 and *The Times Literary Supplement*,
2 July 1931. Virginia Woolf's interest in Elizabeth
Barrett Browning took a somewhat whimsical
turn in *Flush: A Biography* (1933), a reconstruc-
tion of the life of her spaniel.

By one of those ironies of fashion that might have
amused the Brownings themselves, it seems likely that they
are now far better known in the flesh than they have ever
been in the spirit. Passionate lovers, in curls and side
whiskers, oppressed, defiant, eloping – in this guise
thousands of people must know and love the Brownings
who have never read a line of their poetry. They have
become two of the most conspicuous figures in that bright
and animated company of authors who, thanks to our modern habit of writing memoirs and printing letters and sitting
to be photographed, live in the flesh, not merely as of old in
the word; are known by their hats, not merely by their
poems. What damage the art of photography has inflicted
upon the art of literature has yet to be reckoned. How far we
are going to read a poet when we can read about a poet is a
problem to lay before biographers. Meanwhile, nobody can
deny the power of the Brownings to excite our sympathy
and rouse our interest. 'Lady Geraldine's Courtship' is

glanced at perhaps by two professors in American universities once a year; but we all know how Miss Barrett lay on her sofa; how she escaped from the dark house in Wimpole Street one September morning; how she met health and happiness, freedom, and Robert Browning in the church round the corner.

But fate has not been kind to Mrs Browning as a writer. Nobody reads her, nobody discusses her, nobody troubles to put her in her place. One has only to compare her reputation with Christina Rossetti's to trace her decline. Christina Rossetti mounts irresistibly to the first place among English women poets. Elizabeth, so much more loudly applauded during her lifetime, falls farther and farther behind. The primers dismiss her with contumely. Her importance, they say, 'has now become merely historical. Neither education nor association with her husband ever succeeded in teaching her the value of words and a sense of form.' In short, the only place in the mansion of literature that is assigned her is downstairs in the servants' quarters, where, in company with Mrs Hemans, Eliza Cook, Jean Ingelow, Alexander Smith, Edwin Arnold, and Robert Montgomery, she bangs the crockery about and eats vast handfuls of peas on the point of her knife.

If, therefore, we take *Aurora Leigh* from the shelf it is not so much in order to read it as to muse with kindly condescension over this token of bygone fashion, as we toy with the fringes of our grandmothers' mantles and muse over the alabaster models of the Taj Mahal which once adorned their drawing-room tables. But to the Victorians, undoubtedly, the book was very dear. Thirteen editions of *Aurora Leigh* had been demanded by the year 1873. And, to judge from the dedication, Mrs Browning herself was not afraid to say that she set great store by it – 'the most mature of my works', she calls it, 'and the one into which my highest convictions upon Life and Art have entered'. Her letters show that she had had the book in mind for many years. She was brooding over it when she first met Browning, and her intention with regard to it forms almost the first of those confidences about their work which the lovers delighted to share.

> . . . my chief *intention* [she wrote] just now is the writing of a sort of novel-poem . . . running into the midst of our conventions, and rushing into drawing-rooms and the like, 'where angels fear to tread'; and so, meeting face to face and without mask the Humanity of the age, and speaking the truth of it out plainly. That is my intention.

But for reasons which later become clear, she hoarded her intention throughout the ten astonishing years of escape and happiness; and when at last the book appeared in 1856 she might well feel that she had poured into it the best that she had to give. Perhaps the hoarding and the saturation which resulted have something to do with the surprise that awaits us. At any rate we cannot read the first twenty pages of *Aurora Leigh* without becoming aware that the Ancient Mariner who lingers, for unknown reasons, at the porch of one book and not of another has us by the hand, and makes us listen like a three years' child while Mrs Browning pours out in nine volumes of blank verse the story of Aurora Leigh. Speed and energy, forthrightness and complete self-confidence – these are the qualities that hold us enthralled. Floated off our feet by them, we learn how Aurora was the child of an Italian mother 'whose rare blue eyes were shut from seeing her when she was scarcely four years old'. Her father was 'an austere Englishman, Who, after a dry life-time spent at home In college-learning, law and parish talk, Was flooded with a passion unaware', but died too, and the child was sent back to England to be brought up by an aunt. The aunt, of the well-known family of the Leighs, stood upon the hall step of her country house dressed in black to welcome her. Her somewhat narrow forehead was braided tight with brown hair pricked with grey; she had a close, mild mouth; eyes of no colour; and cheeks like roses pressed

135

in books, 'Kept more for ruth than pleasure, – if past bloom, Past fading also'. The lady had lived a quiet life, exercising her Christian gifts upon knitting stockings and stitching petticoats 'because we are of one flesh, after all, and need one flannel'. At her hand Aurora suffered the education that was thought proper for women. She learnt a little French, a little algebra; the internal laws of the Burmese empire; what navigable river joins itself to Lara; what census of the year five was taken at Klagenfurt; also how to draw nereids neatly draped, to spin glass, to stuff birds, and model flowers in wax. For the Aunt liked a woman to be womanly. Of an evening she did cross-stitch and, owing to some mistake in her choice of silk, once embroidered a shepherdess with pink eyes. Under this torture of women's education, the passionate Aurora exclaimed, certain women have died; others pine; a few who have, as Aurora had, 'relations with the unseen', survive, and walk demurely, and are civil to their cousins and listen to the vicar and pour out tea. Aurora herself was blessed with a little room. It was green papered, had a green carpet and there were green curtains to the bed, as if to match the insipid greenery of the English countryside. There she retired; there she read. 'I had found the secret of a garret room Piled high with cases in my father's name, Piled high, packed large, where, creeping in and out . . . like some small nimble mouse between the ribs of a mastodon' she read and read. The mouse indeed (it is the way with Mrs Browning's mice) took wings and soared, for 'It is rather when We gloriously forget ourselves and plunge Soul-forward, headlong, into a book's profound, Impassioned for its beauty and salt of truth – 'Tis then we get the right good from a book'. And so she read and read, until her cousin Romney called to walk with her, or the painter Vincent Carrington, 'whom men judge hardly as bee-bonneted Because he holds that paint a body well you paint a soul by implication', tapped on the window.

This hasty abstract of the first volume of *Aurora Leigh* does it of course no sort of justice; but having gulped down the original much as Aurora herself advises, soul-forward, headlong, we find ourselves in a state where some attempt at the ordering of our multitudinous impressions becomes imperative. The first of these impressions and the most pervasive is the sense of the writer's presence. Through the voice of Aurora the character, the circumstances, the idiosyncrasies of Elizabeth Barrett Browning ring in our ears. Mrs Browning could no more conceal herself than she could control herself, a sign no doubt of imperfection in an artist, but a sign also that life has impinged upon art more than life should. Again and again in the pages we have read, Aurora the fictitious seems to be throwing light upon Elizabeth the actual. The idea of the poem, we must remember, came to her in the early forties, when the con-nexion between a woman's art and a woman's life was unnaturally close, so that it is impossible for the most austere of critics not sometimes to touch the flesh when his eyes should be fixed upon the page. And as everybody knows, the life of Elizabeth Barrett was of a nature to affect the most authentic and individual of gifts. Her mother had died when she was a child; she had read profusely and privately; her favourite brother was drowned; her health broke down; she had been immured by the tyranny of her father in almost conventual seclusion in a bedroom in Wimpole Street. But instead of rehearsing the well-known facts, it is better to read in her own words her own account of the effect they had upon her.

I have lived only inwardly [she wrote] or with *sorrow*, for a strong emotion. Before this seclusion of my illness, I was secluded still, and there are few of the youngest women in the world who have not seen more, heard more, known more, of society, than I, who am scarcely to be called young now. I grew up in the country – I had no social opportunities, had my heart in books and poetry, and my experience in reveries. And so time passed and passed – and afterwards, when my illness came . . . and no prospect (as appeared at one time) of ever passing the threshold of one room again; why then, I turned to thinking with some bitterness . . . that I had stood blind in this temple I was about to leave – that I had seen no Human nature, that my brothers and sisters of the earth were *names* to me, that I had beheld no great mountain or river, nothing in fact. . . . And do you also know what a disadvantage this ignorance is to my art? Why, if I live on and yet do not escape from this seclusion, do you not perceive that I labour under signal disadvantages – that I am, in a manner as a *blind poet*? Certainly, there is compensation to a degree. I have had much of the inner life, and from the habit of self-consciousness and self-analysis, I make great guesses at Human nature in the main. But how willingly I would as a poet exchange some of this lumbering, ponderous, helpless knowledge of books, for some experience of life and man, for some . . .

She breaks off, with three little dots, and we may take advantage of her pause to turn once more to *Aurora Leigh*.

What damage had her life done her as a poet? A great one, we cannot deny. For it is clear, as we turn the pages of *Aurora Leigh* or of the *Letters* – one often echoes the other – that the mind which found its natural expression in this swift and chaotic poem about real men and women was not the mind to profit by solitude. A lyrical, a scholarly, a fastidious mind might have used seclusion and solitude to perfect its powers. Tennyson asked no better than to live with books in the heart of the country. But the mind of Elizabeth Barrett was lively and secular and satirical. She was no scholar. Books were to her not an end in themselves but a substitute for living. She raced through folios because she was forbidden to scamper on the grass. She wrestled with Aeschylus and Plato because it was out of the question that she should argue about politics with live men and women. Her favourite reading as an invalid was Balzac and

George Sand and other 'immortal improprieties' because 'they kept the colour in my life to some degree'. Nothing is more striking when at last she broke the prison bars than the fervour with which she flung herself into the life of the moment. She loved to sit in a café and watch people passing; she loved the arguments, the politics, and the strife of the modern world. The past and its ruins, even the past of Italy and Italian ruins, interested her much less than the theories of Mr Hume the medium, or the politics of Napoleon, Emperor of the French. Italian pictures, Greek poetry, roused in her a clumsy and conventional enthusiasm in strange contrast with the original independence of her mind when it applied itself to actual facts.

Such being her natural bent, it is not surprising that even in the depths of her sick-room her mind turned to modern life as a subject for poetry. She waited, wisely, until her escape had given her some measure of knowledge and proportion. But it cannot be doubted that the long years of seclusion had done her irreparable damage as an artist. She had lived shut off, guessing at what was outside, and inevitably magnifying what was within. The loss of Flush, the spaniel, affected her as the loss of a child might have affected another woman. The tap of ivy on the pane became the thrash of trees in a gale. Every sound was enlarged, every incident exaggerated, for the silence of the sick-room was profound and the monotony of Wimpole Street was intense. When at last she was able to 'rush into drawing-rooms and the like and meet face to face without mask the Humanity of the age and speak the truth of it out plainly', she was too weak to stand the shock. Ordinary daylight, current gossip, the usual traffic of human beings left her exhausted, ecstatic, and dazzled into a state where she saw so much and felt so much that she did not altogether know what she felt or what she saw.

Aurora Leigh, the novel-poem, is not, therefore, the masterpiece that it might have been. Rather it is a masterpiece in embryo; a work whose genius floats diffused and fluctuating in some pre-natal stage waiting the final stroke of creative power to bring it into being. Stimulating and boring, ungainly and eloquent, monstrous and exquisite, all by turns, it overwhelms and bewilders; but, nevertheless, it still commands our interest and inspires our respect. For it becomes clear as we read that, whatever Mrs Browning's faults, she was one of those rare writers who risk themselves adventurously and disinterestedly in an imaginative life which is independent of their private lives and demands to be considered apart from personalities. Her 'intention' survives; the interest of her theory redeems much that is faulty in her practice. Abridged and simplified from Aurora's argument in the fifth book, that theory runs something like this. The true work of poets, she said, is to present their own age, not Charlemagne's. More passion takes place in drawing-rooms than at Roncesvalles with Roland and his knights. 'To flinch from modern varnish, coat or flounce, Cry out for togas and the picturesque, Is fatal – foolish too.' For living art presents and records real life, and the only life we can truly know is our own. But what form, she asks, can a poem on modern life take? The drama is impossible, for only servile and docile plays have any chance of success. Moreover, what we (in 1846) have to say about life is not fit for 'boards, actors, prompters, gaslight, and costume; our stage is now the soul itself'. What then can she do? The problem is difficult, performance is bound to fall short of endeavour, but she has at least wrung her life-blood on to every page of her book, and, for the rest 'Let me think of forms less, and the external. Trust the spirit . . . Keep up the fire and leave the generous flames to shape themselves.' And so the fire blazed and the flames leapt high.

The desire to deal with modern life in poetry was not confined to Miss Barrett. Robert Browning said that he had had the same ambition all his life. Coventry Patmore's 'Angel in the House' and Clough's 'Bothie' were both attempts of the same kind and preceded *Aurora Leigh* by some years. It was natural enough. The novelists were deal-

ing triumphantly with modern life in prose. *Jane Eyre,
Vanity Fair, David Copperfield, Richard Feverel* all trod
fast on each other's heels between the years 1847 and 1860.
The poets may well have felt, with Aurora Leigh, that
modern life had an intensity and a meaning of its own. Why
should these spoils fall solely into the laps of the prose
writers? Why should the poet be forced back to the remote-
ness of Charlemagne and Roland, to the toga and the picturesque, when the humours and tragedies of village life,
drawing-room life, club life, and street life all cried aloud for
celebration? It was true that the old form in which poetry
had dealt with life – the drama – was obsolete; but was
there none other that could take its place? Mrs Browning,
convinced of the divinity of poetry, pondered, seized as
much as she could of actual experience, and then at last threw
down her challenge to the Brontës and the Thackerays
in nine books of blank verse. It was in blank verse that
she sang of Shoreditch and Kensington; of my aunt and the
vicar; of Romney Leigh and Vincent Carrington; of Marian
Erle and Lord Howe; of fashionable weddings and drab
suburban streets, and bonnets and whiskers and four-
wheeled cabs, and railway trains. The poets can treat of
these things, she exclaimed, as well as of knights and dames,
moats and drawbridges and castle courts. But can they? Let
us see what happens to a poet when he poaches upon a
novelist's preserves and gives us not an epic or a lyric but the
story of many lives that move and change and are inspired
by the interests and passions that are ours in the middle of
the reign of Queen Victoria.

In the first place there is the story; a tale has to be told; the
poet must somehow convey to us the necessary information
that his hero has been asked out to dinner. This is a statement that a novelist would convey as quietly and prosaically
as possible; for example, 'While I was kissing her glove,
sadly enough, a note was brought saying that her father sent
his regards and asked me to dine with them next day'. That is
harmless. But the poet has to write:

While thus I grieved, and kissed her glove,
My man brought in her note to say,
Papa had bid her send his love,
And would I dine with them next day!

Which is absurd. The simple words have been made to strut and posture and take on an emphasis which makes them ridiculous. Then again, what will the poet do with dialogue? In modern life, as Mrs Browning indicated when she said that our stage is now the soul, the tongue has superseded the sword. It is in talk that the high moments of life, the shock of character upon character, are defined. But poetry when it tries to follow the words on people's lips is terribly impeded. Listen to Romney in a moment of high emotion talking to his old love Marian about the baby she has borne to another man:

May God so father me, as I do him,
And so forsake me, as I let him feel
He's orphaned haply. Here I take the child
To share my cup, to slumber on my knee,
To play his loudest gambol at my foot,
To hold my finger in the public ways . . .

and so on. Romney, in short, rants and reels like any of those Elizabethan heroes whom Mrs Browning had warned so imperiously out of her modern living-room. Blank verse has proved itself the most remorseless enemy of living speech. Talk tossed up on the surge and swing of the verse becomes high, rhetorical, impassioned; and as talk, since action is ruled out, must go on, the reader's mind stiffens and glazes under the monotony of the rhythm. Following the lilt of her rhythm rather than the emotions of her characters, Mrs Browning is swept on into generalization and declamation. Forced by the nature of her medium, she ignores the slighter, the subtler, the more hidden shades of emotion by which a novelist builds up touch by touch a character in prose. Change and development, the effect of one character upon another – all this is abandoned. The poem becomes one long soliloquy, and the only character that is known to us and the only story that is told us are the character and story of Aurora Leigh herself.

Thus, if Mrs Browning meant by a novel-poem a book in which character is closely and subtly revealed, the relations of many hearts laid bare, and a story unfalteringly unfolded, she failed completely. But if she meant rather to give us a sense of life in general, of people who are unmistakably Victorian, wrestling with the problems of their own time, all brightened, intensified, and compacted by the fire of poetry, she succeeded. Aurora Leigh, with her passionate interest in social questions, her conflict as artist and woman, her longing for knowledge and freedom, is the true daughter of her age. Romney, too, is no less certainly a mid-Victorian gentleman of high ideals who has thought deeply about the social question, and has founded, unfortunately, a phalanstery in Shropshire. The aunt, the antimacassars, and the country house from which Aurora escapes are real enough to fetch high prices in the Tottenham Court Road at this moment. The broader aspects of what it felt like to be a Victorian are seized as surely and stamped as vividly upon us as in any novel by Trollope or Mrs Gaskell.

And indeed if we compare the prose novel and the novel-poem the triumphs are by no means all to the credit of prose. As we rush through page after page of narrative in which a dozen scenes that the novelist would smooth out separately are pressed into one, in which pages of deliberate description are fused into a single line, we cannot help feeling that the poet has outpaced the prose writer. Her page is packed twice as full as his. Characters, too, if they are not shown in conflict but snipped off and summed up with something of the exaggeration of a caricaturist, have a heightened and symbolical significance which prose with its gradual approach cannot rival. The general aspect of things – market, sunset, church – have a brilliance and a continuity, owing to the compressions and elisions of poetry, which mock the prose writer and his slow accumulations of detail. For these reasons *Aurora Leigh* remains, with all its imperfections, a book that still lives and breathes and has its being. And when we think how still and cold the plays of Beddoes or of Sir Henry Taylor lie, in spite of all their beauty, and how seldom in our own day we disturb the repose of the classical dramas of Robert Bridges, we may suspect that Elizabeth Barrett was inspired by a flash of true genius when she rushed into the drawing-room and said that here, where we live and work, is the true place for the poet. At any rate, her courage was justified in her own case. Her bad taste, her tortured ingenuity, her floundering, scrambling, and confused impetuosity have space to spend themselves here without inflicting a deadly wound, while her ardour and abundance, her brilliant descriptive powers, her shrewd and caustic humour, infect us with her own enthusiasm. We laugh, we protest, we complain – it is absurd, it is impossible, we cannot tolerate this exaggeration a moment longer – but, nevertheless, we read to the end enthralled. What more can an author ask? But the best compliment that we can pay *Aurora Leigh* is that it makes us wonder why it has left no successors. Surely the street, the drawing-room, are promising subjects; modern life is worthy of the muse. But the rapid sketch that Elizabeth Barrett Browning threw off when she leapt from her couch and dashed into the drawing-room remains unfinished. The conservatism or the timidity of poets still leaves the chief spoils of modern life to the novelist. We have no novel-poem of the age of George the Fifth.

Mrs Gaskell

Elizabeth Cleghorn Gaskell (1810–65)
This review of Mrs Ellis Chadwick's *Mrs Gaskell:
Haunts, Homes and Stories* was published in *The
Times Literary Supplement*, 29 September 1910.
It is reprinted in *Books and Portraits*.

From what one can gather of Mrs Gaskell's
nature, she would not have liked Mrs Chadwick's book. A
cultivated woman, for whom publicity had no glamour,
with a keen sense of humour and a quick temper, she would
have opened it with a shiver and dropped it with a laugh. It is
delightful to see how cleverly she vanishes. There are no
letters to be had; no gossip; people remember her, but they
seem to have fogotten what she was like. At least, cries Mrs
Chadwick, she must have lived somewhere; houses can be
described. 'There is a long, glass-covered porch, forming a
conservatory, which is the main entrance. . . . On the
ground-floor, to the right, is a large drawing room. On
the left are a billiard room . . . a large kitchen . . . and a
scullery. . . . There are ten bed rooms . . . and a kitchen
garden sufficiently large to supply vegetables for a large
family.' The ghost would feel grateful to the houses; it might
give her a twinge to hear that she had 'got into the best
literary set of the day', but on the other hand it would please

her to read of how Charles Darwin was 'the well-known naturalist'.

The surprising thing is that there should be a public who wishes to know where Mrs Gaskell lived. Curiosity about the houses, the coats, and the pens of Shelley, Peacock, Charlotte Brontë, and George Meredith seems lawful. One imagines that these people did everything in a way of their own; and in such cases a trifle will start the imagination when the whole body of their published writings fails to thrill. But Mrs Gaskell would be the last person to have that peculiarity. One can believe that she prided herself upon doing things as other women did them, only better – that she swept manuscripts off the table lest a visitor should think her odd. She was, we know, the best of housekeepers, 'her standard of comfort', writes Mrs Chadwick, being 'expensive, but her tastes were always refined'; and she kept a cow in her back garden to remind her of the country.

For a moment it seems surprising that we should still be reading her books. The novels of today are so much terser, intenser, and more scientific. Compare the strike in *North and South*, for example, with the *Strife* of Mr Galsworthy. She seems a sympathetic amateur beside a professional in earnest. But this is partly due to a kind of irritation with the methods of mid-Victorian novelists. Nothing would persuade them to concentrate. Able by nature to spin sentence after sentence melodiously, they seem to have left out nothing that they knew how to say. Our ambition, on the other hand, is to put in nothing that need not be there. What we want to be there is the brain and the view of life; the autumnal woods, the history of the whale fishery, and the decline of stage coaching we omit entirely. But by means of comment, dialogues that depart from truth by their wit and not by their pomposity, descriptions fused into a metaphor, we get a world carved out arbitrarily enough by one dominant brain. Every page supplies a little heap of reflections, which, so to speak, we sweep aside from the story and keep to build a philosophy with. There is really nothing to stimulate such industry in the pages of Thackeray, Dickens, Trollope, and Mrs Gaskell. A further deficiency (in modern eyes) is that they lack 'personality'. Cut out a passage and set it apart and it lies unclaimed, unless a trick of rhythm mark it. Yet it may be a merit that personality, the effect not of depth of thought but of the manner of it, should be absent. The tuft of heather that Charlotte Brontë saw was her tuft; Mrs Gaskell's world was a large place, but it was everybody's world.

She waited to begin her first novel until she was thirty-four, driven to write by the death of her baby. A mother, a woman who had seen much of life, her instinct in writing was to sympathize with others. Loving men and women, she seems to have done her best, like a wise parent, to keep her own eccentricities in the background. She would devote the whole of her large mind to understanding. That is why, when one begins to read her, one is dismayed by the lack of cleverness.

Carriages still roll along the streets, concerts are still crowded by subscribers, the shops for expensive luxuries still find daily customers, while the workman loiters away his unemployed time in watching these things, and thinking of the pale, uncomplaining wife at home, and the wailing children asking in vain for enough of food – of the sinking health, of the dying life of those near and dear to him. The contrast is too great. Why should he alone suffer from bad times? I know that this is not really the case; and I know what is the truth in such matters; but what I wish to impress is what the workman feels and thinks.

So she misses the contrast. But by adding detail after detail in this profuse impersonal way she nearly achieves what has not been achieved by all our science. Because they are strange and terrible to us, we always see the poor in stress of some kind, so that the violence of their feeling may break through conventions, and, bringing them rudely into touch with us, do away with the need of subtle understanding. But Mrs Gaskell knows how the poor enjoy themselves; how they visit and gossip and fry bacon and lend each other bits of finery and show off their sores. This is the more remarkable because she was hampered by a refined upbringing and traditions of culture. Her working men and women, her outspoken and crabbed old family domestics, are generally more vigorous than her ladies and gentlemen, as though a touch of coarseness did her good. How admirable, for instance, is the scene when Mrs Boucher is told of her husband's death.

'Hoo mun be told because of th' inquest. See! hoo's coming round; shall you or I do it? Or mappen your father would be best?'

'No; you, you,' said Margaret.

They awaited her perfect recovery in silence. Then the neighbour woman sat down on the floor, and took Mrs Boucher's head and shoulders on her lap.

'Neighbour,' said she, 'your man is dad. Guess yo' how he died?'

'He were drowned,' said Mrs Boucher feebly, beginning to cry for the first time at this rough probing of her sorrow.

'He were found drowned. He were coming home very hopeless o' aught on earth. . . . I'm not saying he did right, and I'm not saying he did wrong. All I say is, may neither me nor mine ever have his sore heart, or we may do like things.'

'He has left me alone wi' a' these children!' moaned the widow, less distressed at the manner of the death than Margaret expected; but it was of a piece with her helpless character to feel his loss as principally affecting herself and her children.

Too great a refinement gives 'Cranford' that prettiness

which is the weakest thing about it, making it, superficially at least, the favourite copy for gentle writers who have hired rooms over the village post-office.

When she was a girl, Mrs Gaskell was famous for her ghost stories. A great story-teller she remained to the end, able always in the middle of the thickest book to make us ask 'What happens next?' Keeping a diary to catch the overflow of life, observing clouds and trees, moving about among numbers of very articulate men and women, high-spirited, observant, and free from bitterness and bigotry, it seems as though the art of writing came to her as easily as an instinct. She had only to let her pen run to shape a novel. When we look at her work in the mass we remember her world, not her individuals. In spite of Lady Ritchie, who hails Molly Gibson 'dearest of heroines, a born lady, unconsciously noble and generous in every thought', in spite of the critic's praise of her 'psychological subtlety', her heroes and heroines remain solid rather than interesting. With all her humour she was seldom witty, and the lack of wit in her character-drawing leaves the edges blunt. These pure heroines, having no such foibles as she loved to draw, no coarseness and no violent passions, depress one like an old acquaintance. One will never get to know them; and that is profoundly sad. One reads her most perhaps because one wishes to have the run of her world. Melt them together and her books compose a large, bright, country town, widely paved, with a great stir of life in the streets and a decorous row of old Georgian houses standing back from the road. 'Leaving behind your husband, children, and civilization, you must come out to barbarism, loneliness, and liberty.' Thus Charlotte Brontë, inviting her to Haworth, compared their lives, and Mrs Gaskell's comment was 'Poor Miss Brontë'. We who never saw her, with her manner 'gay but definite', her beautiful face, and her 'almost perfect arm', find something of the same delight in her books. What a pleasure it is to read them!

George Eliot

George Eliot, pseudonym of Marian Evans
(1819–80)
This article appeared in *The Times Literary
Supplement* of 20 November 1919, and was re-
printed in *The Common Reader:* First Series.
Virginia Woolf also wrote on George Eliot in the
Daily Herald of 9 March 1921 and the *Nation and
Athenaeum* of 30 October 1926.

To read George Eliot attentively is to become
aware how little one knows about her. It is also to become
aware of the credulity, not very creditable to one's insight,
with which, half consciously and partly maliciously, one
had accepted the late Victorian version of a deluded woman
who held phantom sway over subjects even more deluded
than herself. At what moment and by what means her spell
was broken it is difficult to ascertain. Some people attribute
it to the publication of her *Life*. Perhaps George Meredith,
with his phrase about the 'mercurial little showman' and the
'errant woman' on the daïs, gave point and poison to the
arrows of thousands incapable of aiming them so accurately,
but delighted to let fly. She became one of the butts for
youth to laugh at, the convenient symbol of a group of
serious people who were all guilty of the same idolatry and
could be dismissed with the same scorn. Lord Acton had
said that she was greater than Dante; Herbert Spencer
exempted her novels, as if they were not novels, when he

banned all fiction from the London Library. She was the pride and paragon of her sex. Moreover, her private record was not more alluring than her public. Asked to describe an afternoon at the Priory, the story-teller always intimated that the memory of those serious Sunday afternoons had come to tickle his sense of humour. He had been so much alarmed by the grave lady in her low chair; he had been so anxious to say the intelligent thing. Certainly, the talk had been very serious, as a note in the fine clear hand of the great novelist bore witness. It was dated on the Monday morning, and she accused herself of having spoken without due fore-thought of Marivaux when she meant another; but no doubt, she said, her listener had already supplied the correction. Still, the memory of talking about Marivaux to George Eliot on a Sunday afternoon was not a romantic memory. It had faded with the passage of the years. It had not become picturesque.

Indeed, one cannot escape the conviction that the long, heavy face with its expression of serious and sullen and almost equine power has stamped itself depressingly upon the minds of people who remember George Eliot, so that it looks out upon them from her pages. Mr Gosse has lately described her as he saw her driving through London in a victoria:

> a large, thick-set sybil, dreamy and immobile, whose massive features, somewhat grim when seen in profile, were incongruously bordered by a hat, always in the height of Paris fashion, which in those days commonly included an immense ostrich feather.

Lady Ritchie, with equal skill, has left a more intimate indoor portrait:

> She sat by the fire in a beautiful black satin gown, with a green shaded lamp on the table beside her, where I saw German books lying and pamphlets and ivory

151

paper-cutters. She was very quiet and noble, with two steady little eyes and a sweet voice. As I looked I felt her to be a friend, not exactly a personal friend, but a good and benevolent impulse.

A scrap of her talk is preserved. 'We ought to respect our influence,' she said. 'We know by our own experience how very much others affect our lives, and we must remember that we in turn must have the same effect upon others.' Jealously treasured, committed to memory, one can imagine recalling the scene, repeating the words, thirty years later and suddenly, for the first time, bursting into laughter.

In all these records one feels that the recorder, even when he was in the actual presence, kept his distance and kept his head, and never read the novels in later years with the light of a vivid, or puzzling, or beautiful personality dazzling in his eyes. In fiction, where so much of personality is revealed, the absence of charm is a great lack; and her critics, who have been, of course, mostly of the opposite sex, have resented, half consciously perhaps, her deficiency in a quality which is held to be supremely desirable in women. George Eliot was not charming; she was not strongly feminine; she had none of those eccentricities and inequalities of temper which give to so many artists the endearing simplicity of children. One feels that to most people, as to Lady Ritchie, she was 'not exactly a personal friend, but a good and benevolent impulse'. But if we consider these portraits more closely we shall find that they are all the portraits of an elderly celebrated woman, dressed in black satin, driving in her victoria, a woman who has been through her struggle and issued from it with a profound desire to be of use to others, but with no wish for intimacy, save with the little circle who had known her in the days of her youth. We know very little about the days of her youth; but we do know that the culture, the philosophy, the fame, and the influence were all built upon a very humble foundation – she was the granddaughter of a carpenter.

The first volume of her life is a singularly depressing record. In it we see her raising herself with groans and struggles from the intolerable boredom of petty provincial society (her father had risen in the world and become more middle class, but less picturesque) to be the assistant editor of a highly intellectual London review, and the esteemed companion of Herbert Spencer. The stages are painful as she reveals them in the sad soliloquy in which Mr Cross condemned her to tell the story of her life. Marked in early youth as one 'sure to get something up very soon in the way of a clothing club', she proceeded to raise funds for restoring a church by making a chart of ecclesiastical history; and that was followed by a loss of faith which so disturbed her father that he refused to live with her. Next came the struggle with the translation of Strauss, which, dismal and 'soul-stupefying' in itself, can scarcely have been made less so by the usual feminine tasks of ordering a household and nursing a dying father, and the distressing conviction, to one so dependent upon affection, that by becoming a blue-stocking she was forfeiting her brother's respect. 'I used to go about like an owl,' she said, 'to the great disgust of my brother.' 'Poor thing,' wrote a friend who saw her toiling through Strauss with a statue of the risen Christ in front of her, 'I do pity her sometimes, with her pale sickly face and dreadful headaches, and anxiety, too, about her father.' Yet, though we cannot read the story without a strong desire that the stages of her pilgrimage might have been made, if not more easy, at least more beautiful, there is a dogged determination in her advance upon the citadel of culture which raises it above our pity. Her development was very slow and very awkward, but it had the irresistible impetus behind it of a deep-seated and noble ambition. Every obstacle at length was thrust from her path. She knew everyone. She read everything. Her astonishing intellectual vitality had triumphed. Youth was over, but youth had been full of suffering. Then, at the age of thirty-five, at the height of her powers, and in the fulness of her freedom, she made the decision which was of such profound moment to her and still matters even to us, and went to Weimar, alone with George Henry Lewes.

The books which followed so soon after her union testify in the fullest manner to the great liberation which had come to her with personal happiness. In themselves they provide us with a plentiful feast. Yet at the threshold of her literary career one may find in some of the circumstances of her life influences that turned her mind to the past, to the country village, to the quiet and beauty and simplicity of childish memories and away from herself and the present. We understand how it was that her first book was *Scenes of Clerical Life*, and not *Middlemarch*. Her union with Lewes had surrounded her with affection, but in view of the circumstances and of the conventions it had also isolated her. 'I wish it to be understood', she wrote in 1857, 'that I should never invite any one to come and see me who did not ask for the invitation.' She had been 'cut off from what is called the world', she said later, but she did not regret it. By becoming thus marked, first by circumstances and later, inevitably, by her fame, she lost the power to move on equal terms unnoted among her kind; and the loss for a novelist was serious. Still, basking in the light and sunshine of *Scenes of Clerical Life*, feeling the large mature mind spreading itself with a luxurious sense of freedom in the world of her 'remotest past', to speak of loss seems inappropriate. Everything to such a mind was gain. All experience filtered down through layer after layer of perception and reflection, enriching and nourishing. The utmost we can say, in qualifying her attitude towards fiction by what little we know of her life, is that she had taken to heart certain lessons not usually learnt early, if learnt at all, among which, perhaps, the most branded upon her was the melancholy virtue of tolerance; her sympathies are with the everyday lot, and play most happily in dwelling upon the homespun of ordinary joys and sorrows. She has none of that romantic intensity which is connected with a sense of one's own individuality,

154

unsated and unsubdued, cutting its shape sharply upon the background of the world. What were the loves and sorrows of a snuffy old clergyman, dreaming over his whisky, to the fiery egotism of Jane Eyre? The beauty of those first books, *Scenes of Clerical Life, Adam Bede, The Mill on the Floss*, is very great. It is impossible to estimate the merit of the Poysers, the Dodsons, the Gilfils, the Bartons, and the rest with all their surroundings and dependencies, because they have put on flesh and blood and we move among them, now bored, now sympathetic, but always with that unquestioning acceptance of all that they say and do, which we accord to the great originals only. The flood of memory and humour which she pours so spontaneously into one figure, one scene after another, until the whole fabric of ancient rural England is revived, has so much in common with a natural process that it leaves us with little consciousness that there is anything to criticize. We accept; we feel the delicious warmth and release of spirit which the great creative writers alone procure for us. As one comes back to the books after years of absence they pour out, even against our expectation, the same store of energy and heat, so that we want more than anything to idle in the warmth as in the sun beating down from the red orchard wall. If there is an element of unthinking abandonment in thus submitting to the humours of Midland farmers and their wives, that, too, is right in the circumstances. We scarcely wish to analyse what we feel to be so large and deeply human. And when we consider how distant in time the world of Shepperton and Hayslope is, and how remote the minds of farmer and agricultural labourers from those of most of George Eliot's readers, we can only attribute the ease and pleasure with which we ramble from house to smithy, from cottage parlour to rectory garden, to the fact that George Eliot makes us share their lives, not in a spirit of condescension or of curiosity, but in a spirit of sympathy. She is no satirist. The movement of her mind was too slow and cumbersome to lend itself to comedy. But she gathers in her large grasp a great bunch of the main elements of human nature and groups them loosely together with a tolerant and wholesome understanding which, as one finds upon re-reading, has not only kept her figures fresh and free, but has given them an unexpected hold upon our laughter and tears. There is the famous Mrs Poyser. It would have been easy to work her idiosyncrasies to death, and, as it is, perhaps, George Eliot gets her laugh in the same place a little too often. But memory, after the book is shut, brings out, as sometimes in real life, the details and subtleties which some more salient characteristic has prevented us from noticing at the time. We recollect that her health was not good. There were occasions upon which she said nothing at all. She was patience itself with a sick child. She doted upon Totty. Thus one can muse and speculate about the greater number of George Eliot's characters and find, even in the least import-ant, a roominess and margin where those qualities lurk which she has no call to bring from their obscurity.

But in the midst of all this tolerance and sympathy there are, even in the early books, moments of greater stress. Her humour has shown itself broad enough to cover a wide range of fools and failures, mothers and children, dogs and flourishing midland fields, farmers, sagacious or fuddled over their ale, horse-dealers, inn-keepers, curates, and car-penters. Over them all broods a certain romance, the only romance that George Eliot allowed herself – the romance of the past. The books are astonishingly readable and have no trace of pomposity or pretence. But to the reader who holds a large stretch of her early work in view it will become obvious that the mist of recollection gradually withdraws. It is not that her power diminishes, for, to our thinking, it is at its highest in the mature *Middlemarch*, the magnificent book which with all its imperfections is one of the few English novels written for grown-up people. But the world of fields and farms no longer contents her. In real life she had sought her fortunes elsewhere; and though to look back into the past was calming and consoling, there are, even in the early works, traces of that troubled spirit, that exacting and questioning and baffled presence who was George Eliot herself. In *Adam Bede* there is a hint of her in Dinah. She shows herself far more openly and completely in Maggie in *The Mill on the Floss*. She is Janet in *Janet's Repentance*, and Romola, and Dorothea seeking wisdom and finding one scarcely knows what in marriage with Ladislaw. Those who fall foul of George Eliot do so, we incline to think, on account of her heroines; and with good reason; for there is no doubt that they bring out the worst of her, lead her into difficult places, make her self-conscious, didactic, and occasionally vulgar. Yet if you could delete the whole sisterhood you would leave a much smaller and a much inferior world, albeit a world of greater artistic perfection and far superior jollity and comfort. In accounting for her failure, in so far as it was a failure, one recollects that she never wrote a story until she was thirty-seven, and that by the time she was thirty-seven she had come to think of herself with a mixture of pain and something like resentment. For long she preferred not to think of herself at all. Then, when the first flush of creative energy was exhausted and self-confidence had come to her, she wrote more and more from the personal standpoint, but she did so without the unhesitating abandonment of the young. Her self-consciousness is always marked when her heroines say what she herself would have said. She disguised them in every possible way. She granted them beauty and wealth into the bargain; she invented, more improbably, a taste for brandy. But the disconcerting and stimulating fact remained that she was compelled by the very power of her genius to step forth in person upon the quiet bucolic scene.

The noble and beautiful girl who insisted upon being born into the Mill on the Floss is the most obvious example of the ruin which a heroine can strew about her. Humour controls her and keeps her lovable so long as she is small and can be satisfied by eloping with the gipsies or hammering nails into her doll; but she develops; and before George Eliot knows what has happened she has a full-grown woman on her hands demanding what neither gipsies, nor dolls, nor St Ogg's itself is capable of giving her. First Philip Wakem is produced, and later Stephen Guest. The weakness of the one and the coarseness of the other have often been pointed out; but both, in their weakness and coarseness, illustrate not so much George Eliot's inability to draw the portrait of a man, as the uncertainty, the infirmity, and the fumbling which shook her hand when she had to conceive a fit mate for a heroine. She is in the first place driven beyond the home world she knew and loved, and forced to set foot in middle-class drawing-rooms where young men sing all the summer morning and young women sit embroidering smoking-caps for bazaars. She feels herself out of her element, as her clumsy satire of what she calls 'good society' proves.

> Good society has its claret and its velvet carpets, its dinner engagements six weeks deep, its opera, and its faëry ball rooms . . . gets its science done by Faraday and its relig-ion by the superior clergy who are to be met in the best houses; how should it have need of belief and emphasis?

There is no trace of humour or insight there, but only the vindictiveness of a grudge which we feel to be personal in its origin. But terrible as the complexity of our social system is in its demands upon the sympathy and discernment of a novelist straying across the boundaries, Maggie Tulliver did worse than drag George Eliot from her natural surround-ings. She insisted upon the introduction of the great emo-tional scene. She must love; she must despair; she must be drowned clasping her brother in her arms. The more one examines the great emotional scenes the more nervously one anticipates the brewing and gathering and thickening of the cloud which will burst upon our heads at the moment of crisis in a shower of disillusionment and verbosity. It is partly that her hold upon dialogue, when it is not dialect, is slack; and partly that she seems to shrink with an elderly dread of fatigue from the effort of emotional concentration. She allows her heroines to talk too much. She has little verbal felicity. She lacks the unerring taste which chooses one sentence and compresses the heart of the scene within that. 'Whom are you going to dance with?' asked Mr Knightley, at the Westons' ball. 'With you, if you will ask me,' said Emma; and she has said enough. Mrs Casaubon would have talked for an hour and we should have looked out of the window.

Yet, dismiss the heroines without sympathy, confine George Eliot to the agricultural world of her 'remotest past', and you not only diminish her greatness but lose her true flavour. That greatness is here we can have no doubt. The width of the prospect, the large strong outlines of the principal features, the ruddy light of her early books, the searching power and reflective richness of the later tempt us to linger and expatiate beyond our limits. But it is upon the heroines that we would cast a final glance. 'I have always been finding out my religion since I was a little girl,' says Dorothea Casaubon. 'I used to pray so much – now I hardly ever pray. I try not to have desires merely for myself . . .' She is speaking for them all. That is their problem. They cannot live without religion, and they start out on the search for one when they are little girls. Each has the deep feminine passion for goodness, which makes the place where she stands in aspiration and agony the heart of the book – still and cloistered like a place of worship, but that she no longer knows to whom to pray. In learning they seek their goal; in the ordinary tasks of womanhood; in the wider service of their kind. They do not find what they seek, and we cannot wonder. The ancient consciousness of woman, charged with suffering and sensibility, and for so many ages dumb, seems in them to have brimmed and overflowed and uttered a demand for something – they scarcely know what – for something that is perhaps incompatible with the facts of human existence. George Eliot had far too strong an intelligence to tamper with those facts, and

159

too broad a humour to mitigate the truth because it was a stern one. Save for the supreme courage of their endeavour, the struggle ends, for her heroines, in tragedy, or in a compromise that is even more melancholy. But their story is the incomplete version of the story of George Eliot herself. For her, too, the burden and the complexity of womanhood were not enough; she must reach beyond the sanctuary and pluck for herself the strange bright fruits of art and knowledge. Clasping them as few women have ever clasped them, she would not renounce her own inheritance – the difference of view, the difference of standard – nor accept an inappropriate reward. Thus we behold her, a memorable figure, inordinately praised and shrinking from her fame, despondent, reserved, shuddering back into the arms of love as if there alone were satisfaction and, it might be, justification, at the same time reaching out with 'a fastidious yet hungry ambition' for all that life could offer the free and inquiring mind and confronting her feminine aspirations with the real world of men. Triumphant was the issue for her, whatever it may have been for her creations, and as we recollect all that she dared and achieved, how with every obstacle against her – sex and health and convention – she sought more knowledge and more freedom till the body, weighted with its double burden, sank worn out, we must lay upon her grave whatever we have it in our power to bestow of laurel and rose.

'I am Christina Rossetti'

Christina Rossetti (1830–94)
This essay was written in 1930, as a review of the
Life of Christina Rossetti by Mary Sandars and
Christina Rossetti and her Poetry by Edith Birk-
head. It appeared in the *Nation and Athenaeum*,
6 December 1930, and *The Common Reader:*
Second Series. Virginia Woolf had also reviewed
The Family Letters of Christina Rossetti, edited
by William Michael Rossetti, in *The Times Liter-*
ary Supplement of 12 November 1908.

On the fifth of this December Christina Rossetti
will celebrate her centenary, or, more properly speaking,
we shall celebrate it for her, and perhaps not a little to her
distress, for she was one of the shyest of women, and to be
spoken of, as we shall certainly speak of her, would have
caused her acute discomfort. Nevertheless, it is inevitable;
centenaries are inexorable; talk of her we must. We shall
read her life; we shall read her letters; we shall study her
portraits, speculate about her diseases – of which she had a
great variety; and rattle the drawers of her writing-table,
which are for the most part empty. Let us begin with the
biography – for what could be more amusing? As everybody knows, the fascination of reading biographies is irresistible. No sooner have we opened the pages of Miss
Sandars's careful and competent book (*Life of Christina
Rossetti*, by Mary F. Sandars (Hutchinson)) than the old
illusion comes over us. Here is the past and all its in-
habitants miraculously sealed as in a magic tank; all we have

to do is to look and to listen and to listen and to look and soon the little figures – for they are rather under life size – will begin to move and to speak, and as they move we shall arrange them in all sorts of patterns of which they were ignorant, for they thought when they were alive that they could go where they liked; and as they speak we shall read into their sayings all kinds of meanings which never struck them, for they believed when they were alive that they said straight off whatever came into their heads. But once you are in a biography all is different.

Here, then, is Hallam Street, Portland Place, about the year 1830; and here are the Rossettis, an Italian family consisting of father and mother and four small children. The street was unfashionable and the home rather poverty-stricken; but the poverty did not matter, for, being foreigners, the Rossettis did not care much about the customs and conventions of the usual middle-class British family. They kept themselves to themselves, dressed as they liked, entertained Italian exiles, among them organ-grinders and other distressed compatriots, and made ends meet by teaching and writing and other odd jobs. By degrees Christina detached herself from the family group. It is plain that she was a quiet and observant child, with her own way of life already fixed in her head – she was to write – but all the more did she admire the superior competence of her elders. Soon we begin to surround her with a few friends and to endow her with a few characteristics. She detested parties. She dressed anyhow. She liked her brother's friends and little gatherings of young artists and poets who were to reform the world, rather to her amusement, for although so sedate, she was also whimsical and freakish, and liked making fun of people who took themselves with egotistic solemnity. And though she meant to be a poet she had very little of the vanity and stress of young poets; her verses seem to have formed themselves whole and entire in her head, and she did not worry very much what was said of them because in her own mind she knew that they were good. She had also

162

immense powers of admiration – for her mother, for example, who was so quiet, and so sagacious, so simple and so sincere; and for her elder sister Maria, who had no taste for painting or for poetry, but was, for that very reason, perhaps more vigorous and effective in daily life. For example, Maria always refused to visit the Mummy Room at the British Museum because, she said, the Day of Resurrection might suddenly dawn and it would be very unseemly if the corpses had to put on immortality under the gaze of mere sight-seers – a reflection which had not struck Christina, but seemed to her admirable. Here, of course, we, who are outside the tank, enjoy a hearty laugh, but Christina, who is inside the tank and exposed to all its heats and currents, thought her sister's conduct worthy of the highest respect. Indeed, if we look at her a little more closely we shall see that something dark and hard, like a kernel, had already formed in the centre of Christina Rossetti's being.

It was religion, of course. Even when she was quite a girl her lifelong absorption in the relation of the soul with God had taken possession of her. Her sixty-four years might seem outwardly spent in Hallam Street and Endsleigh Gardens and Torrington Square, but in reality she dwelt in some curious region where the spirit strives towards an unseen God – in her case, a dark God, a harsh God – a God who decreed that all the pleasures of the world were hateful to Him. The theatre was hateful, the opera was hateful, nakedness was hateful – when her friend Miss Thompson painted naked figures in her pictures she had to tell Christina that they were fairies, but Christina saw through the imposture – everything in Christina's life radiated from that knot of agony and intensity in the centre. Her belief regulated her life in the smallest particulars. It taught her that chess was wrong, but that whist and cribbage did not matter. But also it interfered in the most tremendous questions of her heart. There was a young painter called James Collinson, and she loved James Collinson and he loved her, but he was a Roman Catholic and so she refused him. Obligingly he became a member of the Church of England, and she accepted him. Vacillating, however, for he was a slippery man, he wobbled back to Rome, and Christina, though it broke her heart and for ever shadowed her life, cancelled the engagement. Years afterwards another, and it seems better founded, prospect of happiness presented itself. Charles Cayley proposed to her. But alas, this abstract and erudite man who shuffled about the world in a state of absent-minded dishabille, and translated the gospel into Iroquois, and asked smart ladies at a party 'whether they were interested in the Gulf Stream', and for a present gave Christina a sea mouse preserved in spirits, was, not unnaturally, a free thinker. Him, too, Christina put from her. Though 'no woman ever loved a man more deeply', she would not be the wife of a sceptic. She who loved the 'obtuse and furry' – the wombats, toads, and mice of the earth – and called Charles Cayley 'my blindest buzzard, my special mole', admitted no moles, wombats, buzzards, or Cayleys to her heaven.

So one might go on looking and listening for ever. There is no limit to the strangeness, amusement, and oddity of the past sealed in a tank. But just as we are wondering which cranny of this extraordinary territory to explore next, the principal figure intervenes. It is as if a fish, whose unconscious gyrations we had been watching in and out of reeds, round and round rocks, suddenly dashed at the glass and broke it. A tea-party is the occasion. For some reason Christina went to a party given by Mrs Virtue Tebbs. What happened there is unknown – perhaps something was said in a casual, frivolous, tea-party way about poetry. At any rate,

suddenly there uprose from a chair and paced forward into the centre of the room a little woman dressed in black, who announced solemnly, 'I am Christina Rossetti!' and having so said, returned to her chair.

With those words the glass is broken. Yes [she seems to say],

I am a poet. You who pretend to honour my centenary are no better than the idle people at Mrs Tebb's tea-party. Here you are rambling among unimportant trifles, rattling my writing-table drawers, making fun of the Mummies and Maria and my love affairs when all I care for you to know is here. Behold this green volume. It is a copy of my collected works. It costs four shillings and sixpence. Read that. And so she returns to her chair.

How absolute and unaccommodating these poets are! Poetry, they say, has nothing to do with life. Mummies and wombats, Hallam Street and omnibuses, James Collinson and Charles Cayley, sea mice and Mrs Virtue Tebbs, Torrington Square and Endsleigh Gardens, even the vagaries of religious belief, are irrelevant, extraneous, superfluous, unreal. It is poetry that matters. The only question of any interest is whether that poetry is good or bad. But this question of poetry, one might point out if only to gain time, is one of the greatest difficulty. Very little of value has been said about poetry since the world began. The judgement of contemporaries is almost always wrong. For example, most of the poems which figure in Christina Rossetti's complete works were rejected by editors. Her annual income from her poetry was for many years about ten pounds. On the other hand the works of Jean Ingelow, as she noted sardonically, went into eight editions. There were, of course, among her contemporaries one or two poets and one or two critics whose judgement must be respectfully consulted. But what very different impressions they seem to gather from the same works – by what different standards they judge! For instance, when Swinburne read her poetry he exclaimed: 'I have always thought that nothing more glorious in poetry has ever been written', and went on to say of her New Year Hymn

that it was touched as with the fire and bathed as in the light of sunbeams, tuned as to chords and cadences of refluent sea-music beyond reach of harp and organ, large echoes of the serene and sonorous tides of heaven.

Then Professor Saintsbury comes with his vast learning, and examines *Goblin Market*, and reports that

> The metre of the principal poem ['Goblin Market'] may be best described as a dedoggerelized Skeltonic, with the gathered music of the various metrical progress since Spenser, utilized in the place of the wooden rattling of the followers of Chaucer. There may be discerned in it the same inclination towards line irregularity which has broken out, at different times, in the Pindaric of the late seventeenth and earlier eighteenth centuries, and in the rhymelessness of Sayers earlier and of Mr Arnold later.

And then there is Sir Walter Raleigh:

> I think she is the best poet alive. . . . The worst of it is you cannot lecture on really pure poetry any more than you can talk about the ingredients of pure water – it is adulterated, methylated, sanded poetry that makes the best lectures. The only thing that Christina makes me want to do, is cry, not lecture.

It would appear, then, that there are at least three schools of criticism: the refluent sea-music school; the line-irregularity school, and the school that bids one not criticize but cry. This is confusing; if we follow them all we shall only come to grief. Better perhaps read for oneself, expose the mind bare to the poem, and transcribe in all its haste and imperfection whatever may be the result of the impact. In this case it might run something as follows: O Christina Rossetti, I have humbly to confess that though I know many of your poems by heart, I have not read your works from cover to cover. I have not followed your course and traced your development. I doubt indeed that you developed very much. You were an instinctive poet. You saw the world from the same angle always. Years and the traffic of the mind with men and books did not affect you in the least. You carefully ignored any book that could shake your faith or any human being who could trouble your instincts. You were wise perhaps. Your instinct was so sure, so direct, so intense that it produced poems that sing like music in one's ears – like a melody by Mozart or an air by Gluck. Yet for all its symmetry, yours was a complex song. When you struck your harp many strings sounded together. Like all instinctives you had a keen sense of the visual beauty of the world. Your poems are full of gold dust and 'sweet geraniums' varied brightness'; your eye noted incessantly how rushes are 'velvet-headed', and lizards have a 'strange metallic mail' – your eye, indeed, observed with a sensual pre-Raphaelite intensity that must have surprised Christina the Anglo-Catholic. But to her you owed perhaps the fixity and sadness of your muse. The pressure of a tremendous faith circles and clamps together these little songs. Perhaps they owe to it their solidity. Certainly they owe to it their sadness – your God was a harsh God, your heavenly crown was set with thorns. No sooner have you feasted on beauty with your eyes than your mind tells you that beauty is vain and beauty passes. Death, oblivion, and rest lap round your songs with their dark wave. And then, incongruously, a sound of scurrying and laughter is heard. There is the patter of animals' feet and the odd guttural notes of rooks and the snufflings of obtuse furry animals grunting and nosing. For you were not a pure saint by any means. You pulled legs; you tweaked noses. You were at war with all humbug and pretence. Modest as you were, still you were drastic, sure of your gift, convinced of your vision. A firm hand pruned your lines; a sharp ear tested their music. Nothing soft, otiose, irrelevant cumbered your pages. In a word, you were an artist. And thus was kept open, even when you wrote idly, tinkling bells for your own diversion, a pathway for the descent of that fiery visitant who came now and then and fused your lines into that indissoluble connection which no hand can put asunder:

> *But bring me poppies brimmed with sleepy death*
> *And ivy choking what it garlandeth*
> *And primroses that open to the moon.*

Indeed so strange is the constitution of things, and so great the miracle of poetry, that some of the poems you wrote in your little back room will be found adhering in perfect symmetry when the Albert Memorial is dust and tinsel. Our remote posterity will be singing:

> *When I am dead, my dearest,*

or:

> *My heart is like a singing bird,*

when Torrington Square is a reef of coral perhaps and the fishes shoot in and out where your bedroom window used to be; or perhaps the forest will have reclaimed those pavements and the wombat and the ratel will be shuffling on soft, uncertain feet among the green undergrowth that will then tangle the area railings. In view of all this, and to return to your biography, had I been present when Mrs Virtue Tebbs gave her party, and had a short elderly woman in black risen to her feet and advanced to the middle of the room, I should certainly have committed some indiscretion – have broken a paper-knife or smashed a tea-cup in the awkward ardour of my admiration when she said, 'I am Christina Rossetti'.

The Compromise

(MRS HUMPHRY WARD)

Mrs Humphry Ward (Mary Augusta Ward)
(1851–1920)
This review of *The Life of Mrs Humphry Ward*,
by her daughter Janet Penrose Trevelyan,
appeared in *The New Republic*, 9 January 1924,
and is reprinted in *Books and Portraits*.

None of the great Victorian reputations has sunk
lower than that of Mrs Humphry Ward. Her novels, already
strangely out of date, hang in the lumber-room of letters like
the mantles of our aunts, and produce in us the same desire
that they do to smash the window and let in the air, to light
the fire and pile the rubbish on top. Some books fade into a
gentle picturesqueness with age. But there is a quality,
perhaps a lack of quality, about the novels of Mrs Ward
which makes it improbable that, however much they fade,
they will ever become picturesque. Their large bunches of
jet, their intricate festoons of ribbon, skilfully and firmly
fabricated as they are, obstinately resist the endearments of
time. But Mrs Trevelyan's life of her mother makes us
consider all this from a different angle. It is an able and
serious book, and like all good biographies so permeates
us with the sense of the presence of a human being that
by the time we have finished it we are more disposed
to ask questions than to pass judgements. Let us

attempt, in a few words, to hand on the dilemma to our readers.

Of Mrs Ward's descent there is no need to speak. She had by birth and temperament all those qualities which fitted her, before she was twenty, to be the friend of Mark Pattison, and 'the best person', in the opinion of J. R. Green, to be asked to contribute a volume to a history of Spain. There was little, even at the age of twenty, that this ardent girl did not know about the Visigothic Invasion or the reign of Alfonso el Sabio. One of her first pieces of writing, A Morning in the Bodleian, records in priggish but burning words her scholar's enthusiasm: '. . . let not the young man reading for his pass, the London copyist, or the British Museum illuminator', hope to enjoy the delights of literature; that deity will only yield her gifts to 'the silent ardour, the thirst, the disinterestedness of the true learner'. With such an inscription above the portal, her fate seems already decided. She will marry a Don, she will rear a small family; she will circulate Plain Facts on Infant Feeding in the Oxford slums; she will help to found Somerville College; she will sit up writing learned articles for the Dictionary of Christian Biography; and at last, after a hard life of unremunerative toil, she will finish the book which fired her fancy as a girl and will go down to posterity as the author of a standard work upon the origins of modern Spain. But, as every one knows, the career which seemed so likely, and would have been so honourable, was interrupted by the melodramatic success of Robert Elsmere. History was entirely forsaken for fiction, and the Origins of Modern Spain became transmuted into the Origins of Modern France, a phantom book which the unfortunate Robert Elsmere never succeeded in writing.

It is here that we begin to scribble in the margin of Mrs Ward's life those endless notes of interrogation. After Robert Elsmere – which we may grant to have been inevitable – we can never cease to ask ourselves, why? Why desert the charming old house in Russell Square for the

170

splendour and expenses of Grosvenor Place? Why wear beautiful dresses, why keep butlers and carriages, why give luncheon parties and week-end parties, why buy a house in the country and pull it down and build it up again, when all this can only be achieved by writing at breathless speed novels which filial piety calls autumnal, but the critic, unfortunately, must call bad? Mrs Ward might have replied that the compromise, if she agreed to call it so, was entirely justified. Who but a coward would refuse, when cheques for £7,000 dropped out of George Smith's pocket before breakfast, to spend the money as the great ladies of the Renaissance would have spent it, upon society and entertainment and philanthropy? Without her novel-writing there would have been no centre for good talk in the pretty room overlooking the grounds of Buckingham Palace. Without her novel-writing thousands of poor children would have ranged the streets unsheltered. It is impossible to remain a schoolgirl in the Bodleian for ever, and, once you breast the complicated currents of modern life at their strongest, there is little time to ask questions, and none to answer them. One thing merges in another; one thing leads to another. After an exhausting At Home in Grosvenor Place, she would snatch a meal and drive off to fight the cause of play centres in Bloomsbury. Her success in that undertaking involved her, against her will, in the anti-suffrage campaign. Then, when the war came, this elderly lady of weak health was selected by the highest authorities to peer into shell-holes, and be taken over men-of-war by admirals. Sometimes, says Mrs Trevelyan, eighty letters were dispatched from Stocks in a single day; five hats were bought in the course of one drive to town – 'on spec., darling'; and what with grandchildren and cousins and friends; what with being kind and being unmethodical and being energetic; what with caring more and more passionately for politics, and finding the meetings of liberal churchmen 'desperately, perhaps disproportionately' interesting, there was only one half-hour in the whole day left for reading Greek.

It is tempting to imagine what the schoolgirl in the Bodleian would have said to her famous successor. 'Literature has no guerdon for bread-students, to quote the expressive German phrase . . . only to the silent ardour, the thirst, the disinterestedness of the true learner, is she prodigal of all good gifts.' But Mrs Humphry Ward, the famous novelist, might have rounded up her critic of twenty. 'It is all very well,' she might have said, 'to accuse me of having wasted my gifts; but the fault lay with you. Yours was the age for seeing visions; and you spent it in dreaming how you stopped the Princess of Wales's runaway horses, and were rewarded by "a command" to appear at Buckingham Palace. It was you who starved my imagination and condemned it to the fatal compromise.' And here the elder lady undoubtedly lays her finger upon the weakness of her own work. For the depressing effects of her books must be attributed to the fact that while her imagination always attempts to soar, it always agrees to perch. That is why we never wish to open them again.

In Mrs Trevelyan's biography these startling discrepancies between youth and age, between ideal and accomplishment, are successfully welded together, as they are in life, by an infinite series of details. She makes it apparent that Mrs Ward was beloved, famous, and prosperous in the highest degree. And if to achieve all this implies some compromise, still – but here we reach the dilemma which we intend to pass on to our readers.

Wilcoxiana

(ELLA WHEELER WILCOX)

Ella Wheeler Wilcox (1850–1919)
This review of *The Worlds and I*, by Ella Wheeler Wilcox, appeared in *The Athenaeum* of 19 September 1919, and is reprinted in *Books and Portraits*.

How can one begin? Where can one leave off? There never was a more difficult book to review. If one puts in the Madame de Staël of Milwaukee, there will be no room for the tea-leaves; if one concentrates upon Helen Pitkin, Raley Husted Bell must be done without. Then all the time there are at least three worlds spinning in and out, and as for Ella Wheeler Wilcox – Mrs Wilcox is indeed the chief problem. It would be easy to make fun of her; equally easy to condescend to her; but it is not at all easy to express what one does feel for her. There is a hint of this complexity in her personal appearance. We write with forty photographs of Mrs Wilcox in front of us. If you omit those with the cats in her arms and the crescent moons in her hair, those stretched on a couch with a book, and those seated on a balustrade between Theodosia Garrison and Rhoda Hero Dunn, all primarily a tribute to the Muse, there remain a number which represent a plump, personable, determined young woman, vain, extremely vivacious, arch, but at the same time sensible, and always in splendid health. She was never a frump at any stage of her career. Rather than look like a blue-stocking, she would have forsaken literature altogether. She stuck a rod between her arms to keep her back straight; she galloped over the country on an old farm horse; she defied her mother and bathed naked; at the height of her fame 'a new stroke in swimming or a new high dive gave me more of a thrill than a new style of verse, great as my devotion to the Muses was, and ever has been'. In short, if one had the pleasure of meeting Mrs Wilcox, one would find her a very well-dressed, vivacious woman of the world. But, alas for the simplicity of the problem! there is not one world but three.

The pre-natal world is indicated rather sketchily. One is given to understand that Mrs Wilcox is appearing for by no means the first time. There have been Ella Wheeler Wilcoxes in Athens and Florence, Rome and Byzantium. She is a recurring, but an improving phenomenon. 'Being an old soul myself,' she says, 'reincarnated many more times than any other member of my family, I knew the truth of spiritual things not revealed to them.' One gift, at least, of supreme importance she brought with her from the shades – 'I was born with unquenchable hope . . . I always expected wonderful things to happen to me.' Without hope, what could she have done? Everything was against her. Her father was an unsuccessful farmer; her mother an embittered woman worn down by a life of child-bearing and hard work; the atmosphere of the home was one of 'discontent and fatigue and irritability'. They lived far out in the country, five miles from a post office, uncomfortably remote even from the dissipations of Milwaukee. Yet Ella Wheeler never lost her belief in an amazing future before her; she was probably never dull for five minutes together. Although acutely aware that her father's taste in hats was distressing, and that the farmhouse walls were without creepers, she had the power within her to transform everything to an object of beauty. The buttercups and daisies of the fields looked to her like rare orchids and hothouse roses. When she was galloping to the post on her farm horse, she expected to be thrown at the feet of a knight, or perhaps the miracle would be reversed and it was into her bosom that the knight would be pitched instead. After a day of domestic drudgery, she would climb a little hill and sit in the sunset and dream. Fame was to come from the East, and love and wealth. (As a matter of fact, she notes, they came from the West.) At any rate something wonderful was bound to happen. 'And I would awaken happy in spite of myself, and put all my previous melancholy into verses – and dollars.' The young woman with the determined mouth never forgot her dollars, and one respects her for saying so. But often Miss Wheeler suggested that in return for what he called her 'heart wails' the editor should send her some object from his prize list – bric-à-brac, tableware, pictures – anything to make the farmhouse more like the house of her dreams. Among the rest came six silver forks, and judge of her emotion! conceive the immeasurable romance of the world! – years later she discovered that the silver forks were made by the firm in which her husband was employed.

But it is time to say something of the poetic gift which brought silver forks from Milwaukee and letters and visits from complete strangers, so that she cannot remember 'any period of my existence when I have not been before the public eye'. She was taught very little; there were odd volumes of Shakespeare, Ouida, and Gauthier scattered about the house, but no complete sets. She did not wish to read, however. Her passion for writing seems to have been a natural instinct – a gift handed down mature from Heaven, and manifesting itself whenever it chose, without much control or direction from Mrs Wilcox herself. Sometimes the Muse would rise to meet an emergency. 'Fetch me a pencil and pad!' she would say, and in the midst of a crowd, to the amazement of the beholders, and to the universal applause, she would dash off precisely the verse required to celebrate the unexpected arrival of General Sherman. Yet sometimes the Muse would obstinately forsake her. What could have been more vexatious than its behaviour in the Hotel Cecil, when Mrs Wilcox wished to write a poem about Queen Victoria's funeral? She had been sent across the Atlantic for that very purpose. Not a word could she write. The newspaper-man was coming for her copy at nine the next morning. She had not put pen to paper when she went to bed. She was in despair. And then at the inconvenient hour of three a.m. the Muse relented. Mrs Wilcox woke with four verses running in her head. 'I felt an immense sense of relief. I knew I could write something the editor would like; something England would like.' And, indeed, 'The Queen's Last Ride' was set to music by a friend of King Edward's, and sung in the presence of the entire Royal family, one of whom afterwards graciously sent her a message of thanks.

Capricious and fanciful, nevertheless the Muse has a heart of gold; she never does desert Mrs Wilcox. Every experience turns, almost of its own accord and at the most unexpected moments, to verse. She goes to stay with friends; she sits next a young widow in the omnibus. She forgets all about it. But as she stands before the looking-glass fastening her white dress in the evening, something whispers to her:

> Laugh and the world laughs with you,
>   Weep and you weep alone,
> For the sad old earth must borrow its mirth,
>   It has trouble enough of its own.

The following morning at the breakfast table I recited the quatrain to the Judge and his wife . . . and the Judge, who was a great Shakespearean scholar said, 'Ella, if you keep the remainder of the poem up to the epigrammatic standard, you will have a literary gem.'

She did keep the poem up to that standard, and two days later he said, 'Ella, that is one of the biggest things you ever did,

176

and you are mistaken in thinking it uneven in merit, it is all good and up to the mark.' Such is the depravity of mankind, however, that a wretched creature called Joyce, belonging to 'the poison-insect order of humanity', as Mrs Wilcox says, afterwards claimed that he had written 'Solitude' himself – written it, too, upon the head of a whisky barrel in a wine-room.

A poetess also was very trying. Mrs Wilcox, who is generosity itself, detected unusual genius in her verse, and fell in love with the idea of playing Fairy Godmother to the provincial poetess. She invited her to stay at an hotel, and gave a party in her honour. Mrs Croly, Mrs Leslie, Robert Ingersoll, Nym Crinkle, and Harriet Webb all came in person. The carriages extended many blocks down the street. Several of the young woman's poems were recited; 'there was some good music and a tasteful supper'. Moreover, each guest, on leaving, was given a piece of ribbon upon which was printed the verse that Mrs Wilcox so much admired. What more could she have done? And yet the ungrateful creature went off with the barest words of thanks; scarcely answered letters; refused to explain her motives, and stayed in New York with an eminent literary man without letting Mrs Wilcox know.

To this day when I see the occasional gems of beauty which still fall from this poet's pen I feel the old wound ache in my heart. . . . Life, however, always supplies a balm after it has wounded us. . . . The spring following this experience my husband selected a larger apartment.

For by this time Ella Wheeler was Wilcox.

She first met Mr Wilcox in a jeweller's shop in Milwaukee. He was engaged in the sterling-silver business, and she had run in to ask the time. Ironically enough she never noticed him. There was Mr Wilcox, a large, handsome man with a Jewish face and a deep bass voice, doing business with the jeweller, and she never noticed his presence. Out she went again, anxious only to be in time for dinner, and thought no more about it. A few days later a very distinguished-looking letter arrived in a blue envelope. Might Mr Wilcox be presented to her? 'I knew it was, according to established ideas, bordering on impropriety, yet I so greatly admired the penmanship and stationery of my would-be acquaintance that I was curious to know more of him.' They corresponded. Mr Wilcox's letters were 'sometimes a bit daring', but never sentimental; and they were always enclosed in envelopes 'of a very beautiful shade', while 'the crest on the paper seemed to lead me away from everything banal and common'. And then the Oriental paper-knife arrived. This had an extraordinary effect upon her such as had hitherto been produced only by reading 'a rare poem, or hearing lovely music, or in the presence of some of Ouida's exotic descriptions'. She went to Chicago and met Mr Wilcox in the flesh. He seemed to her – correctly dressed and very cultured in manner as he was – 'like a man from Mars'. Soon afterwards they were married, and almost immediately Mr Wilcox, to the profound joy of his wife, expressed his belief in the immortality of the soul.

Mrs Wilcox was now established in New York, the admired centre of a circle of 'very worth-while people'. Her dreams in the sunset were very nearly realized. The Bungalow walls were covered with autographs of brilliant writers and the sketches of gifted artists. Universal brotherhood was attempted. It was the rule of the house 'to treat mendicants with sympathy and peddlers with respect'. No one left without 'some little feeling of uplift'. What was wanting? In the first place, 'the highbrows have never had any use for me'. The highbrows could be dispatched with a phrase. 'May you grow at least a sage bush of a heart to embellish your desert of intellect!'

All the same, in her next incarnation she will have nothing to do with genius. 'To be a gifted poet is a glory; to be a worthwhile woman is a greater glory.' There are moments when she wishes that the Muse would leave her at peace.

To be the involuntary mouthpiece of Songs of Purpose, Passion, and Power, greet the war with *Hello, Boys,* and death with Sonnets of Sorrow and Triumph, to feel that at any moment a new gem may form or a fresh cameo compose itself, what fate could be more appalling? Yet such has been the past, and such must be the future, of Ella Wheeler Wilcox.

Olive Schreiner

Olive Schreiner (1855–1920)
This review of *The Letters of Olive Schreiner*,
edited by Cronwright Schreiner, appeared in *The
New Republic*, 18 March 1925.

Olive Schreiner was neither a born letter-writer
nor did she choose to make herself become one. She wrote
carelessly, egotistically, of her health, of her sufferings, of
her beliefs and desires, as if she were talking in the privacy of
her room to a friend whom she trusted. This carelessness,
while it has its charm, imposes some strain on the reader. If
he is not to drop the book, dispirited by the jumble and
muddle of odds and ends, plans and arrangements, bulletins
of health and complaints of landladies – all of which are
related as if Olive Schreiner were a figure of the highest
importance – he must seek some point of view which
imposes unity, some revelation in the light of which this
rather distant and unfamiliar figure becomes of interest. He
will find it perhaps in two sentences written in the same
letter the year before she died. 'Nothing matters in life but
love and a great pity for all our fellows,' she writes. That,
indeed, was her teaching. A few lines lower down she adds,
'It's ten days ago since I've spoken to anyone except the girl

who brings up my coals and water.' That was her fate. The discrepancy between what she desired and what she achieved can be felt, jarring and confusing, throughout the book. Always she is striving for something which escapes her grasp. Always some fault or misfortune interferes with her success. She loves the world at large, but cannot endure any individual in particular. Such would seem to be an outline snapshot of her position. But it is difficult to say further where the fault or the misfortune lay. Early in life she won fame and popularity enough to gratify the most ambitious with her first book, *The Story of an African Farm*. She came to England, and was at once the centre of an appreciative group of distinguished men. Her husband, as he told us last year in his biography, sacrificed a livelihood so that she might pursue her work under the most favourable conditions. She herself had a profound belief in her genius, and an overwhelming enthusiasm for her convictions. Nevertheless, all the strife and agony which ring through her letters – 'The hidden agony of my life no human being understands'; 'I am a fine genius, a celebrity, and tomorrow all these people would tread me under their feet' – resulted in one remarkable novel and a few other fragmentary works which no admirer of *The Story of an African Farm* would care to place beside it. But that famous book itself provides some explanation of her failure to become as she bade fair to become, the equal of our greatest novelists. In its brilliance and power it reminds us inevitably of the Brontë novels. In it, as in them, we feel ourselves in the presence of a powerful nature which can make us see what it saw, and feel what it felt with astounding vividness. But it has the limitations of those egotistical masterpieces without a full measure of their strength. The writer's interests are local, her passions personal, and we cannot help suspecting that she has neither the width nor the strength to enter with sympathy into the experiences of minds differing from her own, or to debate questions calmly and reasonably.

181

Unfortunately for her fame as a writer, it was into debate and politics, and not into thought and literature, that she was impelled, chiefly by her passionate interest in sex questions. She was driven to teach, to dream and prophesy. Questions affecting women, in particular the relations between the sexes, obsessed her. There is scarcely a letter in the present volume in which she does not discuss them with passion, insight, and force, but interminably, in season and out, while her gifts as a writer were bestowed upon a stupendous work upon woman, which, though it took up her time and thought for years, remained, unfortunately, an unfinished masterpiece.

Her private life, disclosed very openly in the present book, seems equally thwarted and disappointed. Driven by asthma to travel perpetually, unrest, dissatisfaction, and, in the end, a profound loneliness, seem to take possession of her. 'I am only a broken and untried possibility,' she wrote. And again, '. . . the only feeling I have about my life is that I have thrown it all away, done nothing with it.' Ironically enough, when she first came to London, her landlady turned her out because she had too many gentlemen visitors; in her last years she was expelled because she had a German name. It is impossible not to feel for her something of the pity and respect which all martyrs inspire in us, and not least those martyrs who are not required to sacrifice their lives to a cause, but sacrifice, perhaps more disastrously, humour and sweetness and sense of proportion. But there were compensations; the cause itself – the emancipation of women – was of the highest importance, and it would be frivolous to dismiss her as a mere crank, a piece of wreckage used and then thrown aside as the cause triumphed onwards. She remains even now, when the vigour of her books is spent, and her personal sway, evidently of the most powerful, is a memory limited to those who knew her, too uncompromising a figure to be so disposed of. Her obsessions and her egotism are perfectly obvious in her letters; but so, too, are her convictions, her ruthless sincerity, and the masterly sanity which so often contrasts on the same page with childish outbursts of unreason. Olive Schreiner was one half of a great writer; a diamond marred by a flaw.

A Terribly Sensitive Mind

(KATHERINE MANSFIELD)

Katherine Mansfield (1890–1923)
This review of *The Journal of Katherine Mansfield, 1914–1922,* appeared in the New York *Herald Tribune* on 18 September 1927. It is reprinted in *Granite and Rainbow.*

The most distinguished writers of short stories in England are agreed, says Mr Murry, that as a writer of short stories Katherine Mansfield was *hors concours.* No one has succeeded her, and no critic has been able to define her quality. But the reader of her journal is well content to let such questions be. It is not the quality of her writing or the degree of her fame that interest us in her diary, but the spectacle of a mind – a terribly sensitive mind – receiving one after another the haphazard impressions of eight years of life. Her diary was a mystical companion. 'Come my unseen, my unknown, let us talk together,' she says on beginning a new volume. In it she noted facts – the weather, an engagement; she sketched scenes; she analysed her character; she described a pigeon or a dream or a conversation, nothing could be more fragmentary; nothing more private. We feel that we are watching a mind which is alone with itself; a mind which has so little thought of an audience that it will make use of a shorthand of its own now and then, or, as the mind in its loneliness tends to do, divide into two and talk to itself. Katherine Mansfield about Katherine Mansfield.

But then as the scraps accumulate we find ourselves giving them, or more probably receiving from Katherine Mansfield herself, a direction. From what point of view is she looking at life as she sits there, terribly sensitive, registering one after another such diverse impressions? She is a writer; a born writer. Everything she feels and hears and sees is not fragmentary and separate; it belongs together as writing. Sometimes the note is directly made for a story. 'Let me remember when I write about that fiddle how it runs up lightly and swings down sorrowful; how it *searches*', she notes. Or, '*Lumbago*. This is a very queer thing. So sudden, so painful, I must remember it when I write about an old man. The start to get up, the pause, the look of fury, and how, lying at night, one seems to get locked.' . . .

Again, the moment itself suddenly puts on significance, and she traces the outline as if to preserve it. 'It's raining, but the air is soft, smoky, warm. Big drops patter on the languid leaves, the tobacco flowers lean over. Now there is a rustle in the ivy. Wingly has appeared from the garden next door; he bounds from the wall. And delicately, lifting his paws, pointing his ears, very afraid the big wave will overtake him, he wades over the lake of green grass.' The Sister of Nazareth, 'showing her pale gums and big discoloured teeth' asks for money. The thin dog. So thin that his body is like 'a cage on four wooden pegs', runs down the street. In some sense, she feels, the thin dog is the street. In all this we seem to be in the midst of unfinished stories; here is a beginning; here an end. They only need a loop of words thrown round them to be complete.

But then the diary is so private and so instinctive that it allows another self to break off from the self that writes and to stand a little apart watching it write. The writing self was a queer self; sometimes nothing would induce it to write. 'There is so much to do and I do so little. Life would be almost perfect here if only when I was *pretending* to work I always was working. Look at the stories that wait and wait just at the threshold . . . *Next day*. Yet take this morning, for instance. I don't want to write anything. It's gray; it's heavy and dull. And short stories seem unreal and not worth doing. I don't want to write; I want to *live*. What does she mean by that? It's not easy to say. But there you are!'

What does she mean by that? No one felt more seriously the importance of writing than she did. In all the pages of her journal, instinctive, rapid as they are, her attitude towards her work is admirable, sane, caustic, and austere. There is no literary gossip; no vanity; no jealousy. Although during her last years she must have been aware of her success she makes no allusion to it. Her own comments upon her work are always penetrating and disparaging. Her stories wanted richness and depth; she was only 'skimming the top – no more'. But writing, the mere expression of things adequately and sensitively, is not enough. It is founded upon something unexpressed; and this something must be solid and entire. Under the desperate pressure of increasing illness she began a curious and difficult search, of which we catch glimpses only and those hard to interpret, after the crystal clearness which is needed if one is to write truthfully. 'Nothing of any worth can come of a disunited being,' she wrote. One must have health in one's self. After five years of struggle she gave up the search after physical health not in despair, but because she thought the malady was of the soul and that the cure lay not in any physical treatment, but in some such 'spiritual brotherhood' as that at Fontainebleau, in which the last months of her life were spent. But before she went she wrote the summing up of her position with which the journal ends.

She wanted health, she wrote; but what did she mean by health? 'By health', she wrote, 'I mean the power to lead a full, adult, living, breathing life in close contact with what I love – the earth and the wonders thereof – the sea – the

186

sun . . . Then I want to *work*. At what? I want so to live that I work with my hands and my feeling and my brain. I want a garden, a small house, grass, animals, books, pictures, music. And out of this, the expression of this, I want to be writing. (Though I may write about cabmen. That's no matter.)' The diary ends with the words 'All is well'. And since she died three months later it is tempting to think that the words stood for some conclusion which illness and the intensity of her own nature drove her to find at an age when most of us are loitering easily among those appearances and impressions, those amusements and sensations, which none had loved better than she.

Dorothy Richardson

Dorothy Richardson (1873–1957)
These reviews of two of the novels in Dorothy
Richardson's sequence *Pilgrimage* appeared in
The Times Literary Supplement of 13 February
1919 and 19 May 1923. They are reprinted in
Contemporary Writers. The review of *Revolving
Lights* was coupled with a discussion of Romer
Wilson's *The Grand Tour,* under the title
'Romance and the Heart'.

The Tunnel

Although *The Tunnel* is the fourth book that
Miss Richardson has written, she must still expect to find
her reviewers paying a great deal of attention to her method.
It is a method that demands attention, as a door whose
handle we wrench ineffectively calls our attention to the fact
that it is locked. There is no slipping smoothly down the
accustomed channels; the first chapters provide an amusing
spectacle of hasty critics seeking them in vain. If this were
the result of perversity, we should think Miss Richardson
more courageous than wise; but being, as we believe, not
wilful but natural, it represents a genuine conviction of the
discrepancy between what she has to say and the form
provided by tradition for her to say it in. She is one of the
rare novelists who believe that the novel is so much alive that
it actually grows. As she makes her advanced critic, Mr
Wilson, remark: 'There will be books with all that cut
out – him and her – all that sort of thing. The book of the

future will be clear of all that.' And Miriam Henderson herself reflects: 'but if books were written like that, sitting down and doing it cleverly and knowing just what you were doing and just how somebody else had done it, there was something wrong, some mannish cleverness that was only half right. To write books knowing all about style would be to become like a man.' So 'him and her' are cut out, and with them goes the odd deliberate business: the chapters that lead up and the chapters that lead down; the characters who are always characteristic; the scenes that are passionate and the scenes that are humorous; the elaborate construction of reality; the conception that shapes and surrounds the whole. All these things are cast away, and there is left, denuded, unsheltered, unbegun and unfinished, the consciousness of Miriam Henderson, the small sensitive lump of matter, half transparent and half opaque, which endlessly reflects and distorts the variegated procession, and is, we are bidden to believe, the source beneath the surface, the very oyster within the shell.

The critic is thus absolved from the necessity of picking out the themes of the story. The reader is not provided with a story; he is invited to embed himself in Miriam Henderson's consciousness, to register one after another, and one on top of another, words, cries, shouts, notes of a violin, fragments of lectures, to follow these impressions as they flicker through Miriam's mind, waking incongruously other thoughts, and plaiting incessantly the many-coloured and innumerable threads of life. But a quotation is better than description.

She was surprised now at her familiarity with the details of the room . . . that idea of visiting places in dreams. It was something more than that . . . all the real part of your life has a real dream in it; some of the real dream part of you coming true. You know in advance when you are really following your life. These things are familiar because reality is here. Coming events cast *light*. It is like dropping everything and walking backward to something you know is there. However far you go out you come back. . . . I am back now where I was before I began trying to do things like other people. I left home to get here. None of those things can touch me here. They are mine.

Here we are thinking, word by word, as Miriam thinks. The method, if triumphant, should make us feel ourselves seated at the centre of another mind, and, according to the artistic gift of the writer, we should perceive in the helter-skelter of flying fragments some unity, significance, or design. That Miss Richardson gets so far as to achieve a sense of reality far greater than that produced by the ordinary means is undoubted. But, then, which reality is it, the superficial or the profound? We have to consider the quality of Miriam Henderson's consciousness, and the extent to which Miss Richardson is able to reveal it. We have to decide whether the flying helter-skelter resolves itself by degrees into a perceptible whole. When we are in a position to make up our minds we cannot deny a slight sense of disappointment. Having sacrificed not merely 'hims and hers', but so many seductive graces of wit and style for the prospect of some new revelation or greater intensity, we still find ourselves distressingly near the surface. Things look much the same as ever. It is certainly a very vivid surface. The consciousness of Miriam takes the reflection of a dentist's room to perfection. Her senses of touch, sight and hearing are all excessively acute. But sensations, impressions, ideas and emotions glance off her, unrelated and unquestioned, without shedding quite as much light as we had hoped into the hidden depths. We find ourselves in the dentist's room, in the street, in the lodging-house bedroom frequently and convincingly; but never, or only for a tantalizing second, in the reality which underlies these appearances. In particular, the figures of other people on whom Miriam casts her capricious light are vivid enough, but their sayings and doings never reach that degree of significance which we, perhaps unreasonably, expect. The old method seems sometimes the more profound and economical of the two. But it must be admitted that we are exacting. We want to be rid of realism, to penetrate without its help into the regions beneath it, and further require that Miss Richardson shall fashion this new material into something which has the shapeliness of the old accepted forms. We are asking too much; but the extent of our asking proves that *The Tunnel* is better in its failure than most books in their success.

Revolving Lights

There is no one word, such as romance or realism, to cover, even roughly, the works of Miss Dorothy Richardson. Their chief characteristic, if an intermittent student be qualified to speak, is one for which we still seek a name. She has invented, or, if she has not invented, developed and applied to her own uses, a sentence which we might call the psychological sentence of the feminine gender. It is of a more elastic fibre than the old, capable of stretching to the extreme, of suspending the frailest particles, of enveloping the vaguest shapes. Other writers of the opposite sex have used sentences of this description and stretched them to the extreme. But there is a difference. Miss Richardson has fashioned her sentence consciously, in order that it may descend to the depths and investigate the crannies of Miriam Henderson's consciousness. It is a woman's sentence, but only in the sense that it is used to describe a woman's mind by a writer who is neither proud nor afraid of anything that she may discover in the psychology of her sex. And therefore we feel that the trophies that Miss Richardson brings to the surface, however we may dispute their size, are undoubtedly genuine. Her discoveries are concerned with states of being and not with states of doing. Miriam is aware of 'life itself'; of the atmosphere of the table rather than of the table; of the silence rather than of the sound. Therefore she adds an element to her perception of things which has not been noticed before, or, if noticed, has been guiltily suppressed. A man might fall dead at her feet (it is not likely), and Miriam might feel that a violent-coloured ray of light was an important element in her consciousness of the tragedy. If she felt it, she would say it. Therefore, in reading *Revolving Lights* we are often made uncomfortable by feeling that the accent upon the emotions has shifted. What was emphatic is smoothed away. What was important to Maggie Tulliver no longer matters to Miriam Henderson. At first, we are ready to say that nothing is important to Miriam Henderson. That is the way we generally retaliate when an artist tells us that the heart is not, as we should like it to be, a stationary body, but a body which moves perpetually, and is thus always standing in a new relation to the emotions which are the same. Chaucer, Donne, Dickens – each if you read him, shows this change of the heart. That is what Miss Richardson is doing on an infinitely smaller scale. Miriam Henderson is pointing to her heart and saying she feels a pain on her right, and not on her left. She points too didactically. Her pain, compared with Maggie Tulliver's, is a very little pain. But, be that as it may, here we have both Miss Wilson and Miss Richardson proving that the novel is not hung upon a nail and festooned with glory, but on the contrary, walks the high road, alive and alert, and brushes shoulders with real men and women.

Royalty

The Story of My Life by Marie, Queen of
Roumania (1875–1938), was published in 1934
and was reviewed by Virginia Woolf in *Time and
Tide* on 1 December. It is reprinted in *The
Moment.*

Many important autobiographies have appeared
this autumn, but none stranger or in certain respects more
interesting than *The Story of My Life*, by Marie, Queen of
Roumania. The reasons seem to be that she is royal; that she
can write; that no royal person has ever been able to write
before; and that the consequences may well be extremely
serious.

Royalty to begin with, merely as an experiment in the
breeding of human nature, is of great psychological interest.
For centuries a certain family has been segregated; bred with
a care only lavished upon race-horses; splendidly housed,
clothed, and fed; abnormally stimulated in some ways,
suppressed in others; worshipped, stared at, and kept shut
up, as lions and tigers are kept, in a beautiful brightly lit
room behind bars. The psychological effect upon them must
be profound; and the effect upon us is as remarkable. Sane
men and women as we are, we cannot rid ourselves of the

superstition that there is something miraculous about these people shut up in their cage. Common sense may deny it; but take common sense for a walk through the streets of London on the Duke of Kent's wedding-day. Not only will he find himself in a minority, but as the gold coach passes and the bride bows, his hand will rise to his head; off will come his hat, or on the contrary it will be rammed firmly on his head. In either case he will recognize the divinity of royalty.

Now one of these royal animals, Queen Marie of Roumania, has done what had never been done before; she has opened the door of the cage and sauntered out into the street. Queen Marie can write; in a second, therefore, the bars are down. Instead of the expected suavities and sweet-nesses we come upon sharp little words; Uncle Bertie laughs, 'his laugh was a sort of crackle'; Kitty Renwick kept the medicine chest; 'the castor oil pills looked like transparent white grapes with the oil moving about inside'; there were 'little squares of burnt skin' on the pudding at Windsor; Queen Victoria's teeth were 'small like those of a mouse'; she had a way of shrugging her shoulders when she laughed; when they rode on the sands at evening 'the shadows become so long that it is as though our horses were walking on stilts'; there was a marvellous stone in the museum, like a large piece of shortbread, that 'swayed slightly up and down when held at one end'. This little girl, in short, smelt, touched, and saw as other children do; but she had an unusual power of following her feeling until she had coined the word for it. That is to say, she can write.

If we want an example of the difference between writing and non-writing we have only to compare a page of Queen Marie with a page of Queen Victoria. The old Queen was, of course, an author. She was forced by the exigencies of her profession to fill an immense number of pages, and some of these have been printed and bound between covers. But between the old Queen and the English language lay an abyss which no depth of passion and no strength of character could cross. Her works make very painful reading on that account. She has to express herself in words; but words will not come to her call. When she feels strongly and tries to say so, it is like hearing an old savage beating with a wooden spoon on a drum. '. . . this last refusal of Servia . . . almost *forces us* to SEE *that* there is *no* false play.' Rhythm is broken; the few poverty-stricken words are bruised and battered; now hooked together with hyphens, now desperately distended with italics and capital letters – it is all no good. In the same way her descriptions of celebrated people slip through the fingers like water. 'I waited a moment in the Drawing-room to speak to Irving and Ellen Terry. He is very gentleman-like, and she, very pleasing and handsome.' This primitive little machine is all that she has with which to register some of the most extraordinary experiences that ever fell to a woman's lot. But probably she owed much of her prestige to her inability to express herself. The majority of her subjects, knowing her through her writing, came to feel that only a woman immune from the usual frailties and passions of human nature could write as Queen Victoria wrote. It added to her royalty.

But now by some freak of fate, which Queen Victoria would have been the first to deplore, her granddaughter, the eldest child of the late Duke and Duchess of Edinburgh, has been born with a pen in her hand. Words do her bidding. Her own account of it is illuminating: 'Even as a child', she says, 'I possessed a vivid imagination and I liked telling stories to my sisters. . . . Then one of my children said to me: "Mama, you ought to write all this down, it is a pity to allow so many beautiful pictures to fade away". . . . I knew nothing whatever about writing, about style or composition, or about the "rules of the game", but I did know how to conjure up beauty, also at times, emotion. I also had a vast store of words.' It is true; she knows nothing about 'the rules of the game'; words descend and bury whole cities under them; sights that should have been seen once and for all are distracted and dissipated; she ruins her effects and muffs her chances; but still because she feels abundantly,

195

because she rides after her emotion fearlessly and takes her fences without caring for falls, she conjures up beauty and conveys emotion. Nor is it merely that by a happy fluke she is able to hit off a moment's impression, a vivid detail; she has the rarer power of sweeping these figures along in a torrent of language; lives grow and change beneath our eyes; scenes form themselves; details arrange themselves; all the actors come alive. Her most remarkable achievement in this way is her portrait of 'Aunty' – that Queen Elizabeth of Roumania who called herself Carmen Sylva. As it happened Queen Victoria also tried her hand at a portrait of this lady. 'The dear charming Queen', she writes, 'came to luncheon . . . She spoke with resignation and courage of her many trials and difficulties . . . I gave her a Celtic brooch and Balmoral shawl, also some books . . . The Queen read to us one of her plays, an ancient Greek story, very tragic. She read it to us most wonderfully and beautifully, and had quite an inspired look as she did so . . . Many could, of course, not understand, as she read it in German, but all were interested.'

In Queen Marie's hands this 'dear charming Queen' develops out of all recognition. She becomes a complex contradictory human being, wearing floating veils and a motoring cap, at once 'splendid and absurd'. We see her posing in bed under a top light; dramatizing herself melodramatically; luxuriating in the flattery of sycophants; declaiming poetry through a megaphone to ships at sea; waving a napkin to grazing cows whom she mistakes for loyal subjects – deluded and fantastic, but at the same time generous and sincere. So the picture shapes itself, until all the different elements are shown in action. Two scenes stand out with genuine vitality – one where the romantic impulsive old lady seeks to enchant an ancient flame – the late Duke of Edinburgh – by dragging him to a hill-top where hidden minstrels spring out from behind rocks and bawl native melodies into his disgusted ears; the other where Queen Elizabeth of Roumania and Queen Emma of Holland sit at their needlework while the Italian secretary reads aloud. He chose Maeterlinck, and as he declaimed the famous passage where the queen bee soars higher and higher in her nuptial ecstasy till at last the male insect, ravaged by passion, drops dismembered to the ground, Carmen Sylva raised her beautiful white hands in rapture. But Queen Emma gave one look at the reader and went on hemming her duster.

Vivid as it all is, nobody is going to claim that Queen Marie ranks with Saint Simon or with Proust. Yet it would be equally absurd to deny that by virtue of her pen she has won her freedom. She is no longer a royal queen in a cage. She ranges the world, free like any other human being to laugh, to scold, to say what she likes, to be what she is. And if she has escaped, so too, thanks to her, have we. Royalty is no longer quite royal. Uncle Bertie, Onkel, Aunty, Nando, and the rest are not mere effigies bowing and smiling, opening bazaars, expressing exalted sentiments, and remembering faces always with the same sweet smile. They are violent and eccentric; charming and ill-tempered; some have bloodshot eyes; others handle flowers with a peculiar tenderness. In short, they are very like ourselves. They live as we do. And the effect is surprising. A month or two ago, the late Duke of Edinburgh was as dead as the dodo. Now, thanks to his daughter, we know that he liked beer; that he liked to sip it while he read his paper; that he hated music; that he loathed Roumanian melodies; and that he sat on a rock in a rage.

But what will be the consequences if this familiarity between them and us increases? Can we go on bowing and curtseying to people who are just like ourselves? Are we not already a little ashamed of the pushing and the staring now that we know from these two stout volumes that one at least of the animals can talk? We begin to wish that the Zoo should be abolished; that the royal animals should be given the run of some wider pasturage – a royal Whipsnade. And another question suggests itself. When a gift for writing lodges in a family, it often persists and improves; and if Queen Marie's descendants improve upon her gift as much as she has improved upon Queen Victoria's is it not quite possible that a real poet will be King of England in a hundred years time? And suppose that among the autumn books of 2034 is *Prometheus Unbound*, by George the Sixth, or *Wuthering Heights*, by Elizabeth the Second, what will be the effect upon their loyal subjects? Will the British Empire survive? Will Buckingham Palace look as solid then as it does now? Words are dangerous things, let us remember. A republic might be brought into being by a poem.

MICHÈLE BARRETT, who has edited and introduced this volume, is a sociologist rather than a literary critic. Her work on Virginia Woolf includes research for a D. Phil thesis, an article on Woolf criticism (*Sociological Review Monograph* No. 26) and a paper (with Jean Radford) on Dorothy Richardson and Virginia Woolf (forthcoming). She teaches in the Department of Social Science and Humanities at The City University in London, is currently working on a general book about Marxist feminist theory and the oppression of women and is a member of the *Feminist Review* collective.